A Season for Healing
A Reason for Hope

Timothy J. O'Brien, M.S.

The 3 Steps To Dealing With Grief

1. Immediate Relief (Audio CD)

2. Compassionate Understanding & Permission to Grieve

3. Adjusting to Your New Way of Living

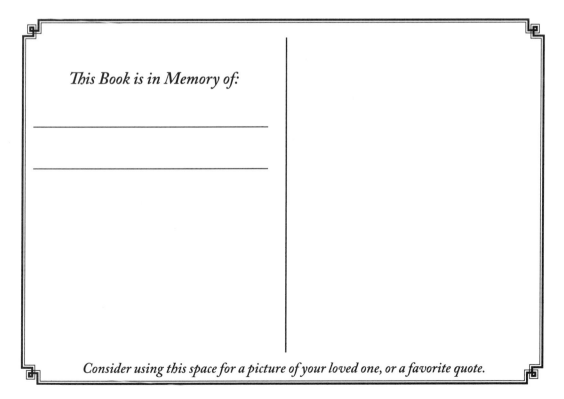

This Book is in Memory of:

_____

_____

Consider using this space for a picture of your loved one, or a favorite quote.

A Season for Healing - A Reason for Hope

I Dedicate This Book To:

Grandma Garner
Dick
Dad & Mom

From the ashes of my mourning for you,
Phoenix-like this program rose.
Thank you

A Season for Healing - A Reason for Hope: The Grief & Mourning Guide and Journal
Library of Congress Control Number: 2010915058
O'Brien, Timothy J.
A Season for Healing - A Reason for Hope: The Grief & Mourning Guide and Journal
/Timothy J. O'Brien;
ISBN 978-0-9845461-0-7
SEL010000 SELF-HELP / Death, Grief, Bereavement
First Printing: September 2010
Published by ISMPI, Inc.
3023 Shannon Lakes N. Suite #102, Tallahassee, FL 32309
© Copyright 2010 by ISMPI, Inc.
Manufactured in the United States of America.
All rights reserved.
Book Layout & Design by: Stacy L. Bagley
Book Printed by Rose Printing Company, Tallahassee, FL

For information about, "A Season for Healing - A Reason for Hope:
The Grief & Mourning Guide and Journal"
please contact ISMPI, Inc. or Timothy J. O'Brien
info@griefguideandjournal.com
tim@griefguideandjournal.com
http://www.griefguideandjournal.com

ISBN: 978-0-9845461-0-7

5 3 4 0 0

9 780984 546107

The 3 Steps to Dealing with Grief

While there are 5 to 7 stages of grief, there are 3 steps to deal with it.

Right now, you might not feel anything at all, and just be numb with the shock of the situation. It is a very uncomfortable feeling, but a very natural reaction to your loss. When you are ready, this program is ready to assist and guide you. **You might start and stop a few times. That's ok; take it at your own pace.**

STEP ONE: Immediate relief, if only temporary, from the physical and emotional stress you're feeling. To get some *immediate relief* from the *stress* that you feel, listen to the CD attached to the back of the book. **Just listen, there is no reading required.** There is a track that will help you calm your mind. **Relief is very important for you now.** And, *The Sleep Technique* should help you fall asleep naturally within about 20 minutes. Natural sleep is nature's way to help keep you healthy.

STEP TWO: Compassionate understanding and giving yourself permission to grieve and mourn. The *"A Season for Healing,"* section of the book, when you are ready, will explain and answer many of the questions and feelings you will have during your time of bereavement. **Journaling** can begin in this section also, if you choose to do it. This section will help you to understand and accept that what you are feeling is both normal and expected.

STEP THREE: Adjusting to your new way of living. The *"A Reason for Hope,"* section of the book explains, in a clear and effective way, steps you can take to help yourself find relief from the physical and emotional stress of grief. And, it will help you as you begin to adjust to life after your loss.

Each of these 3 steps will help you in a different way and at a different time as you grieve and mourn your loss. Grief is a process; it takes time and while some of the "stages" are the same, everyone and every situation is unique and different.

Also, the back of this book contains many useful resources. Use this Guide & Journal and the resources as you travel the journey of grieving the loss of your loved one. *Please take care of yourself and give yourself both permission and time to grieve.*

A Season for Healing – A Reason for Hope

"A Season for Healing – A Reason for Hope" is unique and unlike anything I have seen in my 50 years in Funeral Service. It's not your standard grief therapy. I strongly believe it should be a part of everyone's bereavement."
-- F. James Wylie
Funeral Director, CFSP, former FFDA Executive Director

Introduction:
Take Care of Yourself

Hello, this is Tim O'Brien, author of the Guide and Journal. Having lost both of my parents, my mother-in-law, and a long time business partner all within six years, I can tell you that during times like these there is nothing you can do to remove your pain and sense of loss.

The grief you feel flows from the love and friendship you had with the person who has died. Memories and questions flood the mind and are often overwhelming. These strong, sometimes unrelenting emotions leave you stressed, confused, often numb, tired, and unable to eat, think, sleep, or rest.

Fortunately, thanks to the dedicated work of psychologists, researchers and counselors, there are ways that you can begin to regain control of your life. There are specific effective techniques that can help you calm your mind, steady your emotions, and get restful sleep.

In this program, you will learn many useful ways to help you through this difficult, emotionally exhausting time. These strategies will help you cope with the days ahead. This Guide & Journal can also help others understand the causes of their distress and how to control these feelings.

Share this with them after you've read, listened and learned the techniques that will help you the most.

Because of the special relationship you shared with the person who has died, you will feel and express your loss, sadness, and grief in your own unique and personal way.

I do understand that it is difficult to concentrate right now, however if you'll follow the simple techniques and suggestions you will find strength, not only for yourself, but they can also help you be a source of strength for those who depend on you for guidance and consolation.

Practice the techniques as you read or listen to them and you will find them to be a source of comfort and much needed relief. Even temporary relief will help you remain healthier both mentally and emotionally.

During times of grief and mourning, your normal mental and physical responses and emotions can become exaggerated. You might eat too much or not feel like eating at all. Sleep at night might become difficult or even impossible.

Your normally ordered and quiet mind will probably experience times of turmoil and racing thoughts. And your contacts and conversations with others can become awkward when well-meaning friends and associates, not knowing how to effectively express their sympathy, either hurt you through silence or through poorly chosen expressions.

All of these experiences and events can and do cause serious stress reactions in your mind and body. Sometimes you might become angry. Other times you might become withdrawn or depressed. Your situation can make you feel hopeless. However, there is hope.

There are ways to deal with the extreme stress in your life, right now. You can regain control. It will probably take time, so try to be patient with yourself, and give the suggestions, techniques and time a chance to help you heal.

While dealing with your grief, please realize you do not have to travel the path alone. This program was developed for you as a person, an individual. It can be your companion as you move from day to day, and try to manage the stress and waves of emotions that will ebb and flow like the tides.

However, this Guide & Journal is not intended to be your only resource while you mourn your loss. It is not a substitute for counseling. If you ever feel overwhelmed and in need of assistance in sorting out both your feelings and your personal situation, know that there are many resources available.

Some people will travel the path of bereavement alone. Those who go it alone effectively are few, though.

Most of us will need someone to listen to us and to discuss our situation and options. Friends often fill this need initially. They can truly lend us support and encouragement, especially those friends who have also grieved the loss of a loved one.

Many will find that bereavement or grief support groups are an excellent choice for them. Sharing your experience with those who are walking the same path can be reassuring and comforting.

If the idea of sharing intimate details in a group situation would be difficult or impossible for you, then consider private counseling with a professionally trained grief counselor, therapist or clergy member.

Seeking help is not a sign of weakness. Actually, seeking help to process and manage your grief and mourning experiences is both intelligent and completely appropriate.

Yes, you must experience your grief, in your way, at your pace, that is true. It is also true that you will find there are many compassionate and supportive people and groups ready and very able to assist you. You are not alone.

On page 89 you will find information on:
- The characteristics of a good bereavement group.
- The benefits you can expect to experience if you decide to join a group.
- A list of resources that you can use to find a bereavement group, counselor or therapist in your area.

This Guide and Journal is one significant part of an overall bereavement healing program to help you understand and adjust to your loss. Remember, grief itself, is not a disease, however, if left unresolved, it can cause diseases of both the body and mind. Please take care of yourself. Now, on to the Guide and Journal.

Your Personal Index

As you read the Guide you will probably find certain pages, lines or sections that you would like to find again later. Use this page to note the pages you want to remember, along with a short description of why that page or section is especially meaningful.

It is okay to write in this book. It is designed for you to personalize it.

Page #   Thoughts/Ideas

_____   _____

_____   _____

_____   _____

_____   _____

_____   _____

_____   _____

_____   _____

_____   _____

_____   _____

_____   _____

_____   _____

_____   _____

"It is important for you to realize that what you are experiencing is a normal, natural and expected response to the loss of a significant person in your life."
– Big Bend Hospice, Inc. Tallahassee, Florida

An Overview

About the Grief & Mourning Guide and Journal

We encourage you to use this Guide and Journal to help you understand and express your thoughts, feelings and emotions about the loss of your loved one.

It has four parts:
1. The attached audio CD,
2. The Journal,
3. The Guide,
4. The Techniques, Supplemental Materials, and Additional Resources

The Audio CD

The CD attached inside the front cover contains information that will help you get some immediate relief from the stress of grief. Please be careful: don't listen to these sessions while driving or while doing anything that could be considered dangerous. The first session is an introduction. The second one will make you very relaxed. The third one is designed to put you to sleep.

Session 2 is a twenty-minute guided relaxation session. Find a quiet place where you won't be disturbed for at least twenty minutes while you listen. This session should help you calm your mind and give your body some much needed relaxation. Even if the relief is only temporary at first, it is a valuable process. You are under severe stress as you mourn; your body needs at least periodic times of relaxation for you to remain healthy.

Session 3 is *The Sleep Technique*, a guided relaxation, breathing, and visualizing technique that will help you fall asleep naturally and quickly. Restful sleep is nature's number one restorative power. Give *The Sleep Technique*, a try, you will probably find it really helps. Disrupted sleep is among the most common problems mentioned by the bereaved.

These two short sessions can help you gain some relief starting with the very first time you use them.

The Journal

At the second column of each right-hand page and at the end of the sections, you will find the journal portion of this book. This space is for you to write in, if you want to, as you follow along with the guide. Write whatever you'd like to remember, or possibly think about later.

Some people find journaling very therapeutic, even cathartic. If you find that writing about your experiences is beneficial and you don't have enough room in this book to fully express yourself, consider buying a notebook or blank journal.

The margins in this book will allow you to make notes about ideas you'd like to remember, or jot down any reactions, feelings, and thoughts you have.

Underlining and highlighting specific words or sentences that inspire or motivate you will likely help you get the maximum benefit from this Guide & Journal. There is also a lined page on page xi of this book entitled "Your Personal Index." After you underline or otherwise mark a particular paragraph or page, just put a note on the blank page indicating the page number you want to remember and one or two key words that will help you remember why it is special to you. This will allow you to easily refer to it later.

At the end of the book there is an index of major topics and words. You could also highlight any listing in the index that was of special importance to you. This is another way to make it easy for you to find that page or section later.

This is your book, you can write anything and everything in it that you feel. While writing often helps, not writing anything is all right, too. It is your choice. If you have trouble with the idea of writing in a book, remember this is a Journal too.

The Guide

The next part of this book is the guide portion. In it, you will find information you can use to help you better understand and deal with your bereavement process.

Techniques and Supplemental Materials

In this section you will find detailed explanations and an expanded treatment of ideas and concepts presented in the guide. Here you will find many effective techniques to help you deal with the overwhelming stress caused by the death of your loved one. This section also contains a full explanation of compassion fatigue, a condition that impacts many during times of grief and mourning. You will also find a short narrative by the author concerning his personal bereavement experiences.

There are several acronyms in this book: SMART, BREADS, SAFE, and PAR. These are explained the first time they appear. These words function as tools to help you remember the parts of the related topics they cover.

Additional Resources

You will find additional resources, including a list of books on specific aspects of grieving and related links at the Guide & Journal's website *www.griefguideandjournal.com*

*"For death is no more than a turning
of us over from time to eternity."*
-- William Penn

Step 2:
A Season for Healing

Nothing can replace the loved one you have lost. The death of a spouse is the most severe stress response that we as humans can experience, ranking number one on the Holmes-Rahe Stress Scale. The loss of a family member is number five, relative, close friend or associate is number seventeen. During this time of grief and mourning, while your bereavement crosses through its natural course of cycles and expression, realize that it is important for you to maintain your mental, emotional, and physical health. It is also important for any others who have experienced this loss with you.

To an extent, there is some comfort and solace in knowing that you are not alone. Others who have lost an important person in their life have had similar experiences. However, the feelings you have and the emotions you display are real, genuine and unique. Your way of grieving is an expression of the person you are and that is okay. The range of emotional responses a bereaved person might experience is as wide and varied as the people experiencing them. Normal responses range from shock and denial, to anger, guilt, sadness, anxiety, feelings of isolation, depression, and confusion. You don't have to, and probably won't be able to, conform to anyone else's exact expectations or experiences.

The following pages and the are here to help you in several critical mental, emotional, and physical ways. Please read through the remainder of this guide, write in the journal if you want to, and listen to the CD when suggested. Share this material with anyone else you know who would benefit from it.

Frequency, Intensity and Duration of Episodes

The frequency of grief expressions, their intensity and their duration during the bereavement process, vary from person to person. Each person is unique and grieves in his or her own way. Do not allow anyone else to tell you otherwise. The guidelines presented here should contain something to help everyone. Right now it is probably difficult to think about yourself, or to muster the will to read or listen to anything, but please try. Your health and welfare are important and need attention, even now.

- Frequency is individualistic. The longer term goal is to minimize the frequency of episodes, however, when you do have one, deal with it directly. You certainly don't want to encourage suppression of honest feelings and emotions.

- Intensity, like frequency and duration, will vary episode to episode. At times the intensity of the experience will depend on how tired you are when it occurs. Sometimes, a specific trigger will set a very intense grief episode into motion. Sometimes you simply won't know why a particular experience had such an impact on you; it just happened. All of this is normal.

- Duration is personal, and varies widely among individuals. Also, there are two types of duration to consider. The duration of a single mourning event is one type. Some events might last for days, and others last just a few minutes. The duration of the entire bereavement process is the other type of duration. There is no rule or formula to determine how long your bereavement will last. The best answer sounds like no answer at all. It will last however long it lasts. To some extent, it might never really be over, simply adjusted to over time.

> *"Grief is a process, not a state."*
> *-- Anne Grant*
>
> It is common and expected in America for everyone to be efficient, to be good time managers. That simply won't work with grieving. Be patient with yourself. Be gentle. Your pain is real and there is no quick solution.

Some professionals who deal with those in mourning feel that the overall process averages around a year. Others say it can take from days to months to years. Many feel it is better to think in terms of years instead of days or months.

Over the course of your bereavement, you will probably experience many different emotional responses to the death of your loved one. Normally, you can expect to move from the sensation of intense loss, to periods of anger and rage, through feelings of depression and finally toward hope and recovery. These stages or phases are not clear-cut. They mix, overlap, and sometimes repeat themselves. While grieving, try to live each day the best you can, using all the help and support at your disposal. Eventually, you will notice a change, subtle at first, more pronounced as time passes, that allows you to feel and believe you are returning to a semblance of normal – not the same, never the same, but a new normal, a new way of living, expressing and being.

You should not try to deny the emotions you feel, or suppress them. Again, you do not need to conform to someone else's expectations. If you ever feel overwhelmed or desperate, consider allowing a trusted friend, member of the clergy, or a trained

My Journal

professional to help you through that particular challenge. It is difficult to handle everything alone during normal times; we all need occasional help. It is an indication of wisdom, not weakness, to recognize the benefits of allowing qualified, supportive people to help you during times of bereavement, when necessary.

∞

My Journal

My Journal

"Love is a fabric that never fades, no matter how often
it is washed in the waters of adversity and grief."
-- Anon

Caretakers – Take Care of Yourself Too!

Dealing with Compassion Fatigue

During times of grief and mourning, there are usually one or two people to whom other mourners look for support, guidance and help. These are people who have to remain outwardly strong and supportive, even when they are inwardly grieving their common loss. If you are one of these special people, you might find yourself suffering from more than just your bereavement experiences, which can compound an already challenging problem. This situation is called compassion fatigue. You will find a full explanation of this condition and how to effectively deal with it on page 83.

Stages and Cycles of Grief

Some authors have written about the stages of grief, detailing from five to seven phases, steps or parts. There are authors who deny that stages exist at all, suggesting that grief and mourning are cyclical events that recur, diminishing in intensity over time. There is no need to enter into this debate. Everything that you experience, in your own, unique and often challenging way is all part of the process of dealing with the loss of your loved one. It is an extreme stress event.

What any author writes on this subject, including me, is an attempt to describe the fact that you will experience many types of emotions during your time of bereavement. Some will be intense and sad. Some will be short, possibly funny, and even comforting. There is no accurate way to predict exactly what you will experience, when you will experience it, how long or short the episode will last or what impact it will have on you. Actually, the same or very similar triggering event can have widely different impacts on you depending on factors like where and when the event happens, how rested or tired you are, who is with you, if anyone, and how long it has been since the death of your loved one.

Triggers

Perhaps the most common element among those who grieve is there will be many events, places, people, thoughts and times that will very unexpectedly trigger a grief episode. "One minute I was laughing and fine, then the next minute I was crying and hysterical, I don't know what happened," is an oft repeated, and very normal, expression of surprise after something triggers an event. Anything can trigger an event. Any one of the senses can cause a reaction: the smell of a favorite food, the sound of "our song," the sight of a favorite place.

There are some triggers that won't surprise you, like holidays, birthdays, weddings, anniversaries, special rooms or places, poignant memories of past triumphs and successes with your loved one. The first year following the death is especially difficult for some as each month has its holiday, each season has its special qualities and we as humans plan and celebrate around a calendar of events. These events often mark the treasured memories of our lives. The common advice to wait a year before considering any major changes probably stems from the collective knowledge that every month holds its potential for a new trigger that will send you off on an emotional journey.

The triggers that will surprise you are more subtle. You might go to make a phone call to your loved one, then remember they are no longer available to answer. You might find an old card from you or to you; you'll read it and react very emotionally. You simply can't tell what will trigger an event or when. You can't predict how you will react or how long it will impact you.

Just be aware, that there will very likely be triggering events. When they happen remember they are normal and you should not try to ignore or suppress whatever emotions or thoughts the event produces. Do your best, and try to remember to use some of the techniques you will learn later in this book.

The Circumstances of Death

The circumstances surrounding the death of your loved one and your relationship to/with this important person have a major impact on how his or her death affects you and the frequency, intensity and duration of your grief and mourning episodes.

Was the death sudden and unexpected, or did it occur after a long illness and was therefore expected? Expected and known doesn't mean prepared for – nothing prepares you for the final event of their death. Even if you're a trained professional who deals with bereavement daily, you will still deal with everything humans face after the death of a loved one.

Even having endured the loss of a loved one before, doesn't fully prepare you for another event, another loss. Each loss is unique and will impact you differently. Don't have preconceptions and expectations of

My Journal

what your experience will be like. Grief and mourning seldom conform to our ideas and notions.

With expected death, sometimes there is a sense of relief after a long illness. A sense that it is "finally over" for the person who suffered for so long. Usually this feeling of relief quickly gives way to the sense of loss, the reality that their pain and suffering is over, but in return, they are gone and your pain is still with you.

Tragic deaths, like accidents, murder or suicide can add many more and different levels of emotional trauma to the bereavement process. There can be questions of why, how, who? There can be anger directed at others or even the loved one. If your loved one died from a tragic event consider getting professional counseling assistance to help you sort out your thoughts and feelings, if you have not already. Your funeral director can usually assist you in locating help.

Your mind-set or attitude about the person at the time of their death also impacts you. Were you on good terms? Were there words you wanted to express to the person but didn't? Guilt and remorse over what could have been or should have been said

Written Resources

There are some excellent books covering specific tragic death topics.

These books are not a substitute for counseling if you need it. They are presentations that can often help a person better understand and cope with what happened.

For a list of some of these books visit:

www.griefguideandjournal.com

or reconciled but wasn't, often cause problems beyond the normal feelings of grief. If you are in this situation, again, consider getting help in resolving the issues that concern you. Talking to the person, even though they are gone to this physical realm helps some people. Others sometimes create some type of memorial in their name as a way to allow them to express now what they wished they had expressed before. It is important to admit your feelings and equally important to find ways to effectively deal with them.

Age as a Factor

Many factors influence how we grieve and age is one of them. Being older doesn't necessarily make the death of a loved one easier, especially if this loss is the first major person in the griever's life to die.

If someone has been through the bereavement process before, even more so if they have previously lost a spouse, sibling or child, they have an idea of what to expect. They know how they reacted and responded before. This can help make the process more manageable, not easier. Grief is just not as foreign as it previously was. That said, no two bereavement experiences are the same. Each loss represents a different person, a different time, usually different circumstances. The relationships are never identical. Your feelings, although similar, will not be identical. The benefit of a long life is the many experiences you are able to share and enjoy. An inevitable downside to a very long life is you will, in the natural course of living, have to experience the loss of many friends.

On the other end of the age spectrum, depending on the age and level of maturity, children can experience the loss of a loved one in very different ways than an adult. If there are children impacted by the death of your loved one,

My Journal

pay special attention to them at this time. There are books to help children and young people of all ages understand the bereavement process on their level. Several of these books are listed and reviewed at ***www.griefguideandjournal.com.***

"Am I losing my mind?"

Under normal circumstances, the question, "Am I losing my mind?" is frequently said in jest to a friend. When confronted with the magnitude and finality of death with all of its consequences and ramifications, survivors, overwhelmed by the entirety of the situation, sometimes question their sanity.

Some grief experiences can be too much to experience without help. And, at times like these, when you do feel overwhelmed, out of control or unable to make decisions and act, seek help. The death of your loved one can disorient you, especially if you are in charge of handling any of the arrangements or must make significant decisions quickly. Ask a trusted friend, attorney, member of the clergy or a counselor to help you detail your situation and devise an approach for handling both your feelings and tasks.

Your Relationship

Your relationship with the person who has died will likely be the main determining factor for the course of your bereavement. It will impact the frequency, intensity and duration of your bereavement.

Was this person your mother or father, husband or wife, life partner, brother or sister, child or relative, closest friend or business partner, associate or neighbor? How long you knew them, and how often and how deeply you interacted, are all part of the equation that formulates the experiences you will have.

Cultural Insensitivity

Rituals and traditions
America does not have the type of mourning rituals or prescribed behaviors that many other cultures do. America is a true melting pot of many diverse cultures and therefore

has many different ways of observing grief and mourning. The closest that America, as a country, comes to having a mourning ritual would be the viewing of the body and graveside services. Both of these activities usually take place within a two-day period, and are then over. After these formal, public forums for grieving, you might feel you are on your own.

Many countries and ethnic groups do have very specific grief and mourning practices. Some of these rituals and traditions once had a basis and a practical reason for being that might no longer be necessary, however they are still followed or expected.

Some of the rituals and traditions set forth a sequence of behaviors and a time table for completing the bereavement process. After the completion of the behaviors or the requisite passage of time, the bereaved are expected to "be over it and get on with their lives." This might sound harsh to you, and it might be. The reasoning behind this type of a tradition is often to encourage the person to begin to look towards the rest of his or her life. It is also a reminder of the person's obligations to the survival of the group: sometimes subtle, sometimes blunt.

If you are a member of a group that follows traditional grief and

My Journal

mourning rituals you might find them comforting and a reinforcement of the value of your group and its traditions. If those traditional observances increase your discomfort, consider seeking someone outside of your group to help you through your time of mourning. This is not a suggestion to abandon anything. It is a suggestion to seek assistance in helping you gain a perspective that will best allow you to experience your grief in a way that fits you.

Economic considerations

In the USA we live in an economic-based society – most people must work to maintain the life style they have attained. No work equals no pay, unless you are using vacation or sick leave which run out quickly.

Family leave laws might require time off in certain situations but they do not usually require that the employee be compensated. Insensitivity toward those who grieve and must work can reach the extreme. I am aware of a situation where a company required any employees missing work to attend the funeral of a prominent local citizen to bring in the program from the funeral to prove that missing work was justified.

This need to work often causes severe emotional stress for those who are grieving. You need the money so you have to work however, your heart, head and emotions are distracted. If you must continue to work while you mourn the loss of your loved one, you will find that many of the techniques presented in this book will help you to cope with stress that you feel. Recognize that there will be times at work when you become emotional.

As you work, you will probably find it more difficult to concentrate on your duties. When this happens, be careful, especially if you perform tasks with any degree of danger involved.

While focusing might be difficult, working may actually make time go faster for you. To get through your work day, work in short focused blocks with frequent breaks. Whenever strong memories or emotions begin to overwhelm you,

> *"Every one can master a grief but he that has it."*
> *-- William Shakespeare*
>
> Even your best friends and very well-meaning people can find it awkward to talk with you during your time of loss. Know and accept their good intentions even if how they express themselves falls short.

acknowledge them and write yourself a note about whatever the feelings are and promise you'll give yourself time to experience the episode later. Then, after you are done with work and can be alone for a while, read your notes and allow yourself to experience the emotions. This might sound like an odd suggestion; however, you will find it can work.

Peer pressure and expectations

There are probably individuals or groups you know and associate with who might, consciously or unconsciously, try to impose their concepts, ideas and expectations of how you should grieve, how long it should take and when you should be "over it."

Some of their ideas will be well intended but poorly presented. Other ideas might be well presented but inappropriate for your situation. Most of the time, others want to believe that what worked for them, would work for you and they want to share their thoughts with you. Unfortunately, we are all different and there is no one approach or method that is effective for everyone when dealing with grief.

When it is a close family member or friend offering advice or ideas, they can sometimes be pushy or even aggressive. Often, just listening and saying, "Thank you for your

My Journal

concern," is enough to quiet them. At other times, nothing appears to work. If there are people in your life who interfere with your ability to grieve and mourn in your personal way, consider seeking counseling to help you develop a way to deal with those individuals. It is important that you be able to find the way to mourn that fits you and your personality.

Death is Inconvenient

One of the seldom mentioned aspects of mourning the death of a loved one is how inconvenient it is. Yes, inconvenient. Death just happens, and then you must deal with it on its schedule not yours. Death causes disruptions of your life, dislocations of your plans and then, it might even cause guilt, because you find yourself thinking about yourself and not only about your loved one.

If you find yourself angry with death because it happened when it did, you are not alone. That is a common reaction. One part of you knows that death is inevitable for everyone. Another part of you might wonder, why now and not some other time. Feelings like these are not often expressed because they are considered taboo in American society. If you have these feelings or thoughts, perhaps write about them in the journal. It is okay to feel this way. At some point, you will come to realize that you can't plan everything and not everything will follow your plan.

Multiple or Closely-Occurring Deaths

Dealing with the death of a loved one is difficult. Having to deal with multiple losses at one time or multiple deaths within just days, weeks or months of each other can be overwhelming. When there are multiple deaths at one time, a new array of thoughts and emotions can confront you. Who did you love the most, or can you really differentiate? You might find that the death of one person impacts much harder than the death of another and this can cause questions as to why. The whole spectrum of emotions arises not once, but many times, not all at the same time, and not all with the same frequency, intensity or duration.

In the case of multiple deaths or deaths closely related by time, consider joining a support group or finding counseling help immediately.

These resources can help you to find any additional help or assistance you might need and they can give you a way and a place to express what you are feeling. You have suffered a major loss, and there are trained professionals who can help you deal with it; allow them to.

The Universal Questions

"Where are they now?"

"What happened to them when they died?"

These are the cosmic questions that all humans face especially at the time of a loved one's death. The religious and philosophical thinkers of all cultures have worked to answer these questions. Has anyone ever answered them to everyone's satisfaction? No. Has anyone answered these questions in ways that some have found satisfactory and even consoling? Yes.

Some religions state that a heaven awaits those who live a righteous life. Others believe in the reincarnation of an individual soul until ultimate perfection is realized and it consciously reunites with the Supreme Reality. Others believe that life and individuality ends with death and that we live on through memories,

My Journal

the good deeds we did and the people we influenced in a positive way.

The death of a loved one can strain the limits of those who have firm faith and create a great depression in those who have never embraced a religious way of living. Uncertainty and fear drive many of the thoughts that surround death. Right now is a good time for you to examine what you believe to be true about these important questions. Where do you think your loved one is? What do you believe happened when they died? Use your journal to write your thoughts and ideas if you'd like.

If you have a strong faith, seek guidance and solace with your community of faith. Read and listen to the counsel of the ages and current thought. Attend the ceremonies, and follow the observances of your group.

If you have no set way of viewing what happens at death, consider this as a starting point. Science states in one of its most fundamental laws that energy is neither created nor destroyed, it simply changes form. The extension of this can take many paths. Consider a way to allow this fact to bring you solace and comfort by knowing that the energy that was your loved one on Earth still exists in some form in some way.

Will this last forever?

Based on personal experience and the reported experiences of others, there are several answers to this question. All of the answers are accurate in their own way, even though they might sound contradictory. There are different degrees or shades of duration. Will you ever totally forget your lost loved one? No. Will you ever be able to have a similar type of relationship in the future? Possibly. Do the extreme emotions ever go away? Although time does usually soften the impact of grief, you can never say for certain that you will never have another episode. You might believe you have released some feelings or moved on in some way, however, do not be surprised if an experience somehow triggers a strong emotional response years later. It does happen.

Remember, and be comfortable with the fact that your way of grieving, your way of mourning is usually what is right and good for you. Included in that is how long you grieve and mourn. Some people will appear to be "over it" much faster than others. Do not allow the outer appearance of others to influence you unduly. Bereavement is an internal process, often expressed externally. An outwardly calm looking person might still have extreme inner turmoil and times of strong emotions when alone.

Experience your grief as it comes to you. Know, that for most people, based on the experiences and testimony of millions who have had to mourn before you, that eventually, "the tide turns," and you will notice hope and positive expectations finding their way back into your mind and how you live. Welcome that day when it comes, however, don't try to force its arrival.

A warning and a suggestion are in order here.

Not all ways of expressing grief are healthy.

It is normal to experience changes in your regular eating and sleeping patterns immediately following the loss of a loved one. These disruptions are usually temporary.

However, be on the lookout for radical and prolonged changes in your eating or sleeping patterns.

Be especially careful with alcohol consumption and only take your medications as prescribed.

If you become increasingly depressed or go more than two years without seeing noticeable signs of healing, please seek professional help.

My Journal

"Death ends a life, not a relationship. "
-- Jack Lemmon

Step 3:
A Reason for Hope

The BREADS Formula

There are many pressures that you face while in mourning. Often, these pressures combine to increase your current stress level. However, by setting up a personal stress management program based on the BREADS formula, outlined below, you can reduce the negative effects of stress. While it does take some effort to follow these guidelines and suggestions, you can go as slowly as you would like. This is not a race and the techniques are meant to help, not burden you. It is not easy to take action or try new activities while you mourn your loss. However, your health is important to you and to those who depend on you for support and guidance.

There are six parts to the basic BREADS formula which will help you maintain your health. The first letter of each of the key words, Breathe, Relaxation, Exercise, Attitude, Diet and Sleep spell the word BREADS.

The BREADS formula examines:
- how you breathe,
- the regular use of relaxation techniques,
- exercise or active movement,
- monitoring your attitude,
- maintaining a balanced diet, and
- getting enough natural restful sleep.

After you have read through all six components, consider which one would be the easiest for you to remember and practice right now. Do not attempt all six at once; take small steps. After you have used one technique or suggestion for a while, try another one. Be gentle with yourself.

When you use this six-part approach to working with your grief responses, you can help your body and mind counteract some of the strong emotions you are experiencing. At times, nothing may help very much. You might feel temporarily overwhelmed by the wave of feelings which seemingly resist your efforts to modify them. However, by paying attention to each of these six areas, you should be able to cope with your thoughts and emotions better. Your grief episodes won't stop happening. Your painful feelings won't go completely away. You'll just be better able to recognize what is happening and you'll be equipped to deal with them.

Breathing

Breathing correctly is very important. That sounds like an odd statement. Even though breathing happens naturally without our conscious involvement, it is possible to breathe incorrectly. Basically, there are two types of breathing: chest breathing and stomach or diaphragm breathing. When you breathe with your chest you stimulate your sympathetic nervous system and breathe less deeply. When you breathe with your diaphragm, you calm yourself by breathing deeply, using your lungs more efficiently and activating your parasympathetic nervous system.

When you feel drowsy or depressed, consciously breathe with your chest, holding your stomach still. Breathe slightly faster than you normally do. Five or ten minutes of breathing like this should stimulate you into a more alert state. Don't hyperventilate, and if this type of breathing makes you dizzy, stop immediately.

When you feel excited, angry, or agitated, remind yourself to breathe with your stomach. Keep your chest and shoulders still and allow your stomach to move in and out as you breathe.

The important point to remember about your breathing is this: breath follows awareness and, awareness follows breath. Breathing is normally an unconscious action, where the situation directs the rate of breathing. But it can be a conscious act, where you direct the rate and thereby control your body's response. Remember: shallow chest breathing stimulates, deep stomach breathing calms and quiets.

Relaxation

Relaxation techniques include a wide range of activities. The important points to remember about using relaxation techniques are variety and regularity. One of the purposes of using relaxation techniques is to break routine, or to break patterns of thinking and behavior temporarily. Taking a walk, reading an entertaining book, expressing yourself through art or music, or starting a new hobby can all qualify as relaxation techniques if they give you some relief from your normal thoughts and concerns.

Unfortunately, you can't store the benefits of relaxation. You will need to do something relaxing everyday, sometimes more often, to keep enjoying the benefits. Don't overdo it, though. Ten to fifteen minutes will be enough to help clear your mind and strengthen the body by de-stressing it.

In the techniques section of this guide, you will learn more than twenty relaxation techniques for you to consider using. Remember, more is not necessarily better. One or two techniques done correctly and regularly will give you the relief you seek.

Meditation, or the Relaxation Response as it is also called, is an effective relaxation technique that helps to calm and center the mind.

My Journal

Session 2 of the audio CD is a twenty minute, guided relaxation session. Try it the next time you feel tense or have difficulty slowing down the thoughts racing through your mind. Simply place the CD into a CD player, play Session 2, and follow the easy instructions. It really is that simple. You will feel much different in just twenty minutes.

Exercise

Exercise: Please, don't let the word exercise make you nervous or uneasy. Exercise offers many benefits and one of the most important is that it helps to strengthen the immune system. It can also help to relieve the tension and stress of anxiety and depression, which so many people experience as part of their grieving process. Physical activity helps balance the mind and body and helps us sleep better. Getting started can be as easy as taking a short walk. This can also count as one of your relaxation techniques.

Exercising might be the least of your concerns right now. You might feel there is no way at all to make yourself get up and move. However, because of its many physical and mental benefits, please consider it. If you've never exercised before, simply walking on a regular basis in the beginning will produce benefits for you. If you normally exercise, make yourself keep it up now, even if it is a reduced workout, a little exercise is better than no exercise. If you're new to exercising, ask your doctor for advice on how to start a basic aerobic exercise program.

The keys to success with exercise are moderation and consistency. You want to start very slowly and work up to a more strenuous routine over a period of two to three months. A little exercise and light stretching everyday is better than trying to fit a week's worth of effort into one or two sessions.

> *Remember. . .*
>
> Before you begin any exercise program, or radically change your diet, make an appointment with your physician for a physical exam to ensure you are able to safely start an exercise or diet routine.

What are the reasons to exercise?

1. To strengthen the heart and muscles of the body,
2. To help your metabolism work more efficiently, supporting a healthy weight,
3. To increase mental clarity and your ability to concentrate,
4. To improve sleep, and
5. To increase flexibility and endurance.

Those are five compelling reasons to exercise three or four times per week for twenty to thirty minutes. A simple way to remember the elements of a complete exercise routine is the word S.A.F.E = Strength, Aerobic and Flexibility Exercises.

Attitude

Attitude plays a part in every thought, decision, and response you have. It plays a major role when dealing with grief.

Anhedonia is the scientific name for a very common symptom of bereavement and expressions of grief. It is the inability to find enjoyment in what are normally enjoyable events like family gatherings and other activities which one usually likes. It is a loss of pleasurable feelings.

It is a strong case of lethargy. It is the loss of interest in many aspects of life. It is a shift away from

---

My Journal

---

caring, concern, and active mental involvement. It is a change in attitude, normally temporary, toward the activities of life. It is also a very normal response to the death of a significant person in your life. These feelings might surprise you; however, they are common and actually somewhat expected. You have experienced an extreme event. Many of your plans and hopes for the future could now be in question. This type of situation and these types of concerns can have a profound and lasting impact on you.

During bereavement, many conflicting emotions and thoughts may occur. You might not want to be alone, but you'd prefer that those around you were just there and didn't speak. Or, you might recognize the fact that you are pushing yourself too hard to keep busy, but you don't want to experience all the racing thoughts and vivid memories that surface if you stop being active.

Depression and feeling negative can actually produce chemicals that weaken the immune system. And, a weakened immune system is the doorway for disease. So, it is important to try and minimize the impact of any episodes of depression. This six-part program we have been describing will help you deal with depression.

Episodes of depression or anger or resentment are expected, normal

---

Personal Insight

After the death of his wife, British author C. S. Lewis described it this way:
"No one ever told me about the laziness of grief... I loathe the slightest effort. Not only writing, but even reading a letter is too much."

His book *A Grief Observed* is an insightful record of his bereavement experiences from the time immediately following his loss until his rediscovery of hope. It is an intimate history of the many stages/phases of grief common to the bereavement process.

A Grief Observed, and other books on grief and mourning, are listed at

www.griefguideandjournal.com.

---

and usually temporary. Understanding that can make it easier to experience them. If you find that your times of depression, anger, or other strong emotions begin to last longer or become more intense over time, consider discussing the situation with your funeral director, physician, clergy, hospice worker or a counselor.

Again, it is a sign of intelligence to consult with and use professional help for challenges in any area of life. Competent help is available.

During your time of bereavement it is important to adjust to your loss while developing a balance between sharing time and experiences with others and spending time alone to sort through your thoughts and feelings.

Medical and psychological research shows that having a strong social support network is a beneficial factor for the health and longevity of those who have experienced the death of someone important to them, especially for men.

It is a very good idea to share the information in this guide with a person who is supporting you during your time of bereavement. See if they would like to practice the techniques you choose with you; they will benefit from them also. And, if you have trouble motivating yourself to try the suggestions in this book, you could also ask a supportive friend to gently remind and encourage you.

Realize and expect that people can be clumsy and inappropriate at times with their comments. You will probably notice that some people avoid you because they feel awkward and don't know how to talk to you. Others will try, with great feelings, to

My Journal

say something that they hope will help you and it will come out all wrong. However, don't let this stop you from interacting with others. And, if you find yourself becoming reclusive, try to break the pattern, even if you don't feel like it. Try to reach a balance between time with others and time alone.

It is important to be natural. Don't deny or avoid any of the emotions or thoughts that come to you. Try to observe them. Understand that your mind is trying to adjust to the finality of a very traumatic experience: death. Platitudes, poems and purely motivational information might be inappropriate and ineffective. However, if a particular book, phrase, passage, or poem does gives you solace, comfort or hope, keep it around and refer to it often. It is your choice, not someone else's.

When it comes to grief and mourning experiences, we as humans are both very much alike and very different. Alike in that there are many common emotions we experience. Different in that the frequency, intensity and duration of our bereavement experiences will vary among us just like each snowflake is slightly different from every other. The commonality helps us gain understanding from the words and experiences of others. Our differences

mean that we each must find our personal direction and timing for passing through the bereavement process.

If your physician has prescribed medication for you, or if you are working with a counselor, be certain to follow his or her instructions exactly. If you have any questions about the medication or the course of your counseling, discuss it with your doctor or counselor. Clear communication is important to effective results.

There is one final condition relating to attitude that must be mentioned. **Alexithymia** is "a condition of human brain and personality development in which an individual is unable to express emotions or feelings in words." (Steven Locke, M.D., *The Healer Within*).

Some people, even when they experience a great loss, cannot explain in detail how deeply they feel about the event. While they feel it inside, they can't verbalize or express it. Others

> *"There is a sacredness in tears. They are not the mark of weakness, but of power. They speak more eloquently than ten thousand tongues. They are the messengers of overwhelming grief... and unspeakable love."*
> *-- Washington Irving*

might misinterpret their inability to express themselves as indifference or coldness, and frustration or hard feelings can follow. Be aware that this condition exists, and if you experience it, consider discussing it with your funeral director or a counselor. If someone appears to have difficulty understanding how deeply you feel about your loss, remember that they might be experiencing this condition.

Diet

Diet refers to what you eat, not just what you do to lose weight. Look at food as fuel for the body and mind: the muscles, bones, nerves, and brain cells. Just as a car won't run without gasoline, and won't run very well with poor quality gasoline, your body needs proper nutrition several times daily to stay healthy. To a large extent, you really are what you eat.

Often, during bereavement, people lose their appetite. A few go on eating binges, but under-eating or sporadic eating appears to be more common.

When you are upset, feel uncertain, worried, or angry, thinking about a balanced diet can be difficult. If you know you are not eating correctly, set an alarm or ask someone to remind you to eat even when you don't feel like it. Go to the grocery

My Journal

store and buy complete ready-to-heat-and-serve meals to make it easier for you to get the nutrients you need. Or, if you eat out, use the alarm to help you remember it is time to go eat.

During bereavement, time often appears to move in an uneven way. Certain events will feel as if they pass quickly. And others will seem to take forever. This dislocation of the sense of time makes it difficult to regulate our body clocks for eating and sleeping. Using an alarm clock or other people as a reminder can help you return to a regular eating schedule.

If you just don't feel like eating, try to eat at least a small portion at each meal time and try to eat small amounts more often. Also, select balanced foods that you like and have them around. It is easier to eat something you like. Be careful, though.

Junk food earned its name; it doesn't have the nutrients your body needs to remain strong.

With diet, like exercise, consistency and moderation are important. Your body can't store all the reserves it needs. You must replenish it with wholesome foods several times a day for your immune and other systems to remain strong. Good nutrition is especially important during the severe strain of bereavement. During times of extreme stress, the body actually has increased requirements for remaining strong. If you take daily vitamins, don't forget them! Or, if you don't, ask your doctor if he or she thinks they would benefit you.

If you need help knowing what a balanced diet is, ask your physician or contact a nutritionist to help you.

Sleep

Sleep: Right now, it is important that you get enough restful sleep. It is nature's number one restorative power. When uncontrolled memories flood the mind, or when the body feels tense and anxious, sleep might be difficult or impossible. However, it is important to try and maintain good sleep habits. Session 3 of the attached CD, *The Sleep Technique,* should help you get some rest by allowing you to fall asleep naturally within about twenty minutes.

Summary & Suggestions

The death of a significant person in your life is the strongest stress event you can experience. You can begin to effectively deal with all of the physical, mental and emotional challenges of mourning by using the six-part **BREADS** formula. These six components are:

1. Pay attention to how you **B**reathe. Use your chest and shoulders when you need stimulation and use your diaphragm or stomach when you need to relax.

2. Use **R**elaxation techniques on a regular basis to help develop and maintain a mind/body balance. The techniques section of this guide along with the CD will help you learn and practice these helpful techniques.

3. You receive many important benefits from regular aerobic **E**xercise. If new to exercise, check with your doctor before starting an exercise program. Begin slowly and build up the frequency, duration, and intensity of your exercise program over several months. If you already have an exercise program, stick with it.

4. Recognize that **A**ttitude affects many aspects of life. Your thoughts, decisions, and responses are filtered through your attitude. Remember that the many emotions you feel, their intensity and frequency, are all part of your natural reaction to the death of someone important to you. Try to strike a balance

My Journal

between spending time alone with your thoughts and feelings, and spending time with others.

5. Eat a balanced **D**iet. Your food is the only fuel your body has to power itself and keep healthy.

6. Get restful **S**leep: This is often difficult during times of grief and mourning; however, it is important to do your best to insure you get enough restful sleep. *The Sleep Technique,* Session 3 of the attached CD, should help you.

If you feel overwhelmed by or, uninformed about any aspect of your life, find someone to help you get a sense of control over your situation. You might ask your funeral director to help you locate an appropriate professional to help you meet your challenges. It is also a good idea to ask others you trust to help you find and contact these professionals.

Understand that your grief is a legitimate expression of your feelings over losing someone significant. There are no quick fixes or immediate cures for the pain, confusion, or other emotions you might be feeling right now.

The length of bereavement varies from person to person. It passes through phases and lasts from just a few months for some, to several years for others. The length of your bereavement will be an expression of your uniqueness. You need not compare it to some standard from a book or to others.

Have hope, accept the expressions of love and support from others, no matter how awkward, and try to rebuild your life. While your life can never be the same as it was before your loss, the testimony of many who have gone through this experience before you, including me, is that there are ways to begin again. There are ways to find hope, meaning and purpose in life again.

Additional Resources

This Guide & Journal contains specific, detailed information to help you approach the loss of your loved one. It is designed to support you as you walk through the most significant experience and stress related event that one can face. Knowing that each person is unique and that how you experience and express your grief will be different, there are many additional resources for you to consider at *www.griefguideandjournal.com.*

My Journal

"To live in the hearts we leave behind is not to die."
--Thomas Campbell

An Expanded Explanation of Stress and How it Affects You

The Techniques Section

Since the loss of your loved one is the biggest stress response your body will ever experience, we are now going to enter into more detail on how to handle this stress. If you feel unsure about anything we have covered so far, review the previous section before moving on to the advanced techniques.

This section will cover, in detail, what stress really is, how it affects you and what you can do to lessen its negative impact on you and those around you. This presentation is specific and direct in an attempt to avoid any confusion or misunderstanding that indirect writing might cause. This section will give you the tools you need to begin to regain control of your life. Do not allow the number of techniques to overwhelm or frustrate you. Simply try one or two that sound good or that you feel will help you the most. Over time, you can try some of the other ideas and suggestions. Try some of these techniques, but be easy on yourself.

The areas covered will be:

1. The causes and effects of stress,
2. Specific stress management techniques,
3. A thorough explanation of Meditation & the Relaxation Response,
4. An overview of sleep (nature's number one stress management tool), and
5. The eight keys to good sleep.

Some of these parts are technical because, if you want to be able to deal with and eventually control the stress in your life, it is important that you fully understand what stress is and why it impacts you so strongly.

The Causes and Effects of Stress

Stress is technically a prolonged imbalance of the autonomic nervous system. This imbalance eventually wears down our immune system making us susceptible to sickness. Dr. Hans Selye gives us an easily understandable definition of stress as the "rate of wear and tear on our bodies." Stress doesn't cause illness directly, it weakens our natural defenses and then we become sick.

Our mind and nervous system are inspiring creations. They are also intricate and can be somewhat confusing. We must understand the path of stress, how it develops, and how we sustain it.

The most common example of stress is what Dr. Hans Selye identifies as the "fight or flight response." When we perceive a situation or event as threatening, the cerebral cortex region of our brain sends an electrical signal to the brain stem. This electrical impulse stimulates our sympathetic nervous system into dominance. With this stimulation, many chemical reactions take place in our body.

Adrenalin spurts into our system. Our pulse and breathing rate increase. Our pupils dilate and our sense of awareness sharpens. We are now ready to fight or take flight. In times of real need and threats to our safety, this is a highly appropriate response by the body.

After the threat passes or we recognize that the situation is not dangerous, our system, if allowed, will enter a natural recovery stage. Our parasympathetic system, the other half of the autonomic system, will start to balance the sympathetic imbalance that has occurred.

The body seeks a state of balance called homeostasis. This occurs when the sympathetic and parasympathetic parts of the

> *"The risk of love is loss, and the price of loss is grief -- But the pain of grief is only a shadow when compared with the pain of never risking love."*
> *-- Hilary Stanton Zunin*

autonomic system are in a balanced state of operation, periodically alternating temporary dominance (i.e., "taking turns") based on the body's needs at the time.

Stress occurs when these systems remain in a habitual state of imbalance. We then find ourselves in a near constant state of arousal or withdrawal and the recovery phase is not expressed fully to rebalance our system. This is what happens while you grieve the death of your loved one. One side of your nervous system gets "stuck on," and wears you down. This causes chronic chemical imbalances. These chemicals, coupled with a fatigued mental state, weaken our immune system. When this happens, we are vulnerable. Diseases that we once easily avoided now infect us. Glaser and Glaser at Ohio State University discovered that under stress our bodies produce fewer T-cells to combat disease. These T-cells are our natural defense barriers against the bacteria and viruses that invade our bodies.

Stress related diseases strike at our weakest point. For some, it will be constant gastrointestinal disturbances. For others, it will be high blood pressure or high cholesterol levels, or, catching every bug going around.

We all experience internal and external stimulations that can lead to

My Journal

stress, especially during times of grief. These stimulations are opportunities to act or react. How we respond to these events determines the level of stress we perceive. If we balance times of extreme stimulation with regular opportunities to relax and recover, stress will have less impact.

There are two key points to remember about maintaining balance and avoiding the effects of stress.

First, the "fight or flight response" was developed in humans when we had to worry about escaping animals that might eat us. Today, saber-tooth tigers are extinct but the response isn't. Worry, doubt, fear, or hearing bad news can elicit the same physical response that the hungry tiger once provoked. There is an important difference between these two situations. When the tiger chased us in antiquity and when we exercise correctly today a special situation exists. We experience alignment when our mental expectation, our physical preparation and our opportunity to express are all appropriate and in balance. The tiger scared us. Our body mobilized and we ran. Once we were safe, we rested and recovered.

This alignment is often difficult in the work or family environment under normal conditions. It is a severe challenge during times of grief and mourning. When people or events

> *"Mourning is one of the most profound human experiences that it is possible to have... The deep capacity to weep for the loss of a loved one and to continue to treasure the memory of that loss is one of our noblest human traits".*
> *-- Shneidman*

This quote eloquently encapsulates what it is to be human. We have the deep and lasting ability to love, to care, to share, and to recognize the profound nature of a major loss. The death of a loved one is the most profound human experience.

cause a stress response, we can seldom express our self efficiently enough to avoid residual stress symptoms. In these situations we need to either learn to experience the events without reacting or we need to learn and practice effective Stress Management And Relaxation Techniques (SMART) to allow full recovery.

The word PAR, or P.A.R, represents the second key to attaining and maintaining balance. It defines our only choice and chance to control the stress in our life. It stands for our Perception, Attitude and Response. We have one chance to avoid stress: at the time of our initial perception. After our cerebral cortex signals a response to the brain stem, it is all neurochemistry from there on, and beyond our control for that episode. If we don't like a particular response we make or, if through habit, we allow an unconscious response, we can start a counteractive response to offset the first inappropriate one. However, we can't change or alter that first reaction.

This relationship between perception, attitude and response explains why death is such a debilitating stress response and why it is so difficult to deal with. Perceptions come from all directions, often as memories and often quickly and intensely. Your normal attitude and responses can become exaggerated, confused and even conflicted. These unrelenting thoughts and emotions wear you down and recovering, especially if you still have responsibilities to others, does not seem possible. During times like these, try to remember one or two of the techniques you will learn to help you experience at least temporary relief.

Our life is the total effect of our responses. If we want to experience a change in our life, we must change our attitude. We filter our perceptions through our attitudes. This directly affects the responses that our body makes. Perception plus attitude equals response. We can't change the world, but we can change

My Journal

our response to it. We change our responses by changing our attitude. It takes relearning, practice and time. However, eventually, we can develop new, lower stress attitudes.

Please realize that in this context, attitude means much more than just being positive or negative. Our attitude, as expressed by our behavior and response patterns, includes our basic frame of reference that guides our actions. Psychologists call this our paradigm. Underlying this frame of reference is our level of self-esteem and ultimately our basic beliefs about the world and universe around us. When we have a strong foundation based on core beliefs about our place in the scheme of the universe, it is easier to have a positive self-concept, which is the combination of our self-image and self-esteem. We then can accept ourselves as being good and worthy. Since we love and care about ourselves and want to improve our situation, we make the effort to do so. When faced with the loss of a loved one, your core beliefs might be challenged or you might question them. The techniques in this guide will help you develop a way to find new guidance in your life.

Stress is often the result of unresolved conflicts, of either a physical, mental or emotional origin. While you grieve you will probably experience many of these conflicts. They are actually what constitute the bereavement process. Dealing with them will present you with both challenges and opportunities. Realize that what you are feeling is natural. Be gentle with yourself. Do the best you can in each situation and seek help for those times and events you feel you cannot handle alone.

Specific Stress Management Techniques

We have already reviewed what stress is, along with its main causes and possible negative side effects. Now we are going to examine specific techniques you can use to release the stress in your life.

We will divide these techniques into two main groups: the mental techniques and the physical techniques. The mental techniques focus primarily on the psychological causes of stress. The physical techniques give you tools to use on the effects of stress. Both are important to an effective SMART program. However, you will see, as your mental techniques strengthen, the need for some of the physical techniques will decline. Once you release the causes of your stress, the symptoms will normally diminish or disappear completely.

Stress takes place in the mind and manifests in the body and our behavior. When we have our perceptions, attitudes, and responses aligned and in harmony, we act effectively and stress plays a minor role in our life. When they get out of balance, especially in severe, extreme cases like the death of a loved one, stress occurs and we need methods for dealing with it. We will start with the mental techniques. The following suggestions can help you release the sources of stress in your life.

Mental Techniques

1. **Above all, be conscious.** Learn to notice when you are in stressful situations. Then you can learn to contain and eventually release them. When you become aware of what triggers your grief episodes, you can begin to both control and eventually eliminate the stress they cause.

2. **View yourself in a holistic way.** You are a complex being, made of many interactive parts. Unless you approach the decisions in your life from this understanding, your plans will be incomplete. Seek to balance the spiritual, mental, emotional, physical, financial and social parts of you.

My Journal

3. **Know and admit that dealing with the loss of your loved one is a challenge, while trying to maintain a positive mental attitude.** Believe that you will eventually begin to feel better. Expect that you will be able to deal with your grief. Know that there is a way to maintain health. Keep looking for that way until you find it.

   If you accept responsibility for your life and your experiences, that will help you to maintain your clarity. You cannot control what happens to you; however, you can exert a degree of control over how you react and respond to your experiences. The research of Dr. Martin Seligman has shown in controlled studies over a twenty-five year period that optimism produces more positive results than pessimism. An excellent book discussing that research is Dr. Seligman's *Learned Optimism*.

4. **Try to isolate the stress that you feel.** Keep the stress from one area of your life from spilling over into another if you can. Although that is what usually happens and we experience angst or generalized anxiety, it does not need to be that way. Without separation, there is no relief and the exhaustion stage of stress begins. While it is difficult to stop thinking, wondering and worrying at times, effective stress management urges us to learn that skill.

   A useful tool for helping you learn this is to write out your worries or concerns. That is one of the reasons I have included a journal area in this book. List in detail every aspect, challenge or problem and the options you feel are in front of you. Write out what you believe the worst case outcome could be, and then brainstorm five potential solutions to that worst case scenario. By writing out the details of your worries and concerns, you can make them more manageable and reduce their power over you.

   Remember the acronym **QTIP** and try to **Q**uit **T**aking **I**t **P**ersonally. When someone says something that hurts or upsets you, or if you feel others are being insensitive, try to let inappropriate comments and actions pass you by. Take a deep breath, and try to let the feelings pass or weaken. If you allow the words or actions of others to negatively impact you, you suffer, not the person who spoke or acted

> *"Death leaves a heartache no one can heal, love leaves a memory no one can steal."*
> *-- From a headstone in Ireland*

inappropriately. Work to accept people as they are and adjust your responses to them. Don't just tolerate them and waste emotional energy. Once you know and understand this difference between acceptance and tolerance, your SMART program will be both easier to exercise and more effective.

Everyone has demands and difficult people to deal with. Develop an effective plan of action to handle these. Francis of Assisi, the 12th century Italian mystic, expresses an effective SMART program in three short sentences: *"Grant me the serenity to accept what I cannot change. The courage to change what I can, and the wisdom to know the difference."* Dr. Mihaly Csikszentmihalyi (pronounced "Chick cent me hi"), the former chairman of the Psychology Department at the University of Chicago in his psychologically significant book *Flow: The Psychology of Optimal Experience*, states that we have a choice.

He explains that we can learn to control consciousness and live a fulfilling life, or we can try in vain to control our environment and fail, because we have allowed others to dictate the course of our life. The death of your loved one has created sadness, uncertainty,

My Journal

confusion and many other emotions. Regaining some control over your life and experiences is difficult, but worth the effort.

5. **Also, have compassion for others, even as you appreciate it from them.** The old saying tells us to walk a mile in someone else's shoes. As you seek to understand another's point of view, you will probably find that it helps you in your recovery process. Anthony Robbins, a popular and effective Peak Performance Consultant says, *"Remember, no matter how thin you slice a piece of bread, it still has two sides."* There are always at least two angles to every situation. We exist in a dualistic reality. Be open to diversity of opinion and as free from preconceptions as possible.

6. **Stay organized and have set routines for repetitive work.** This will keep you from becoming overwhelmed while you mourn. See routines as a way to provide normalcy for your life. They also help you standardize what you do, saving time and making it less likely that you will misplace something.

7. **Although you might not feel it is possible, allow yourself to enjoy some leisure time and activities.** This is crucial to the recovery process. Set aside time regularly, daily is the ideal, and use it just for

> *"To spare oneself from grief at all cost can be achieved only at the price of total detachment, which excludes the ability to experience happiness"*
> *-- Erich Fromm*

you. This will revitalize you and help you maintain a better perspective. Even spending fifteen minutes per day is effective.

8. **Develop a hobby if you don't have one.** Learn to quilt, take yoga or dance classes, try gardening, or play a musical instrument. Make the activity different from the regular routine that causes you stress or reminds you in any way of your lost loved one. Try to use the opposite side of your brain, too. Engaging in artistic activities uses your right brain while analytical pursuits engage your left brain. This will help balance your mind and nervous system.

9. **Reduce the number of activities that you do.** Our lives have become complex because we continually add new demands on our time. While you mourn especially, you don't need extra pressures or demands. Do some mental house cleaning and drop old, impractical or ineffective habits and attitudes. Try to drop the unnecessary, combine where practical and

delegate the trivial and repetitious.

10. **Have a friend and be a friend. Find someone who you can talk to without fear or hesitation.** They can help you clarify your thinking and release pent up feelings. Be careful with this friend, in two ways. First, if you want to vent anger, sadness or frustration, ask permission before you begin. And second, be sure that you are as eager to listen and help them when they need it. *"Do unto others as you would have them do unto you,"* really is the golden rule for friendships. Research has repeatedly shown that humans are happiest when talking and interacting with other humans. Friends and support groups are especially important while you grieve.

11. **Reduce debt and simplify your finances if you can.** A significant amount of the stress and anxiety people experience relates in some way to money. If the death of your loved one has or will cause financial turmoil for you, seek assistance. Find someone who can help you understand your current financial position and help you develop a plan for the immediate and distant future. The added stress of financial concerns can exaggerate the emotions you already feel.

My Journal

The Physical Techniques

The physical techniques we will now cover are effective at teaching you how to relax and will temporarily relieve and reduce your stress. However, don't allow them to be the only part of your SMART program. These techniques work primarily on the symptoms of stress. Balance is the key to an effective program. You use the physical techniques for immediate relief while you work to make the mental changes necessary, to stop and release the root causes of the stress in your life.

An important key to success with these techniques is conscious effort. Old habits can hurt us. Being conscious of our actions allows us to exercise control in our life. Now here are the physical techniques.

Alternate Nostril Breathing

This very simple process calms the mind and increases our ability to concentrate. Practice it right now as you read to this explanation. The ability to focus and concentrate is very important during the turmoil caused by the death of your loved one.

Gently hold your left nostril closed with your left thumb and breathe in through your right nostril. Then immediately close your right nostril with your left ring finger, release your left thumb, and exhale evenly through your left nostril. Then breathe in through your left nostril. Now, calmly close the left nostril again with your left thumb and exhale through the right side. This is one complete round of alternate nostril breathing. It is very simple and highly effective.

Remember to breathe in evenly and use your diaphragm, allowing your stomach to expand and contract. Your inhalations and exhalations should be about the same length. Don't hold your breath; just breathe

---

CD Session 3

In the segment entitled *"Overview of Sleep"* and *"The Eight Keys to Good Sleep,"* found a little later in this book, we will review steps you can take during your waking hours to improve the quality and restfulness of your sleep.

Session 3 of the attached CD presents *The Sleep Technique* itself. It is an effective relaxation and visualization technique that allows natural sleep to occur within twenty minutes by removing the obstacles that sometimes prevent it.

calmly and easily, alternating sides. Do five or six rounds every morning and evening or any time you want to calm down or focus quickly.

Just concentrate on your breathing. Let it be even, calm and slightly deeper than normal. Remember to breathe with your stomach like you learned in the first part of this presentation. Deep, diaphragmatic breathing coupled with alternate nostril breathing, will balance and relax you deeply.

Get enough rest

Adequate, restful, natural sleep revitalizes our brain and nervous system. This is an important part of reducing stress. Fatigue and nervousness add to our stress. The old saying *"every hour of sleep before midnight is worth two after midnight"* emphasizes the need for quality sleep. Mental fatigue, sadness and depression lower the quality and quantity of work we produce. Adequate sleep and regular time for yourself help us to perform with maximum efficiency.

HILL

This next technique might sound silly, however, please try it.

Remember the word HILL and *"hold it loosely, Lenny."* Notice how you hold your pen or should I say for

My Journal

most people I know, how you clutch it. If someone can pull the pen from between your fingers with little effort then you're doing fine. However, if you are holding it the way a child hangs on to a prized toy, it is a source of physical tension.

Sit straight when you write or use your computer. Breathe deeply with your stomach and hold your pen or pencil like it was an egg, something fragile. When working at your computer, try to rest your hands and palms in a way that allows your arms and shoulders to relax. Check your shoulders too, make sure they are in a relaxed position. If you do this, your shoulders will relax and the source of many afternoon headaches will vanish.

If you ever feel tension building in your hands, wrists, arms or shoulders, take a thirty-second break. Check your breathing, and then slowly roll your head in a circle several times in both directions and gently roll your shoulders forward and backward. Also have several "private little joys" that you can use to escape momentarily from the rigors of routine. This could be a special picture or a gem stone that you keep in your drawer or on your desk. Use these little joys to remind you of a pleasant time in your life. That might be very difficult right now as you mourn your loss, however,

---

Music Therapy

The American Music Therapy Association has a very interesting website at:

www.musictherapy.org

Some of the benefits the association lists for music therapy are:

- promote wellness
- manage stress
- alleviate pain
- express feelings
- enhance memory
- improve communication
- promote physical rehabilitation

---

these ideas only work when you make them a part of your regular routine. You are not trying to deny your loss or your feelings; you simply want to find ways to set them aside for a while so your mental and physical systems can recuperate, and you can stay healthy.

Listen to soothing music or natural sounds at low decibel levels. Pounding rhythms and loud sounds stimulate our nervous system and can increase stress. Music Therapy, was once thought to be false or fake medicine, now there are university degrees and careers available in music therapy.

Silence

Also, periodically consider silence as an alternate stress management technique. Many people have difficulty with silence. While you mourn your loss, being "alone with your thoughts," might be unsettling or even frightening. However, do make quiet time part of your bereavement process. Quiet time, without music or other distractions, allows your mind to sort through and begin to make sense of all the contrasting and possibly conflicting thoughts and emotions you feel.

A way to help reduce these strong emotions and still benefit from periodic silence is to experience your quiet time outside when possible. Sunlight helps you to absorb vitamin D and is a natural remedy for depression and seasonal affective disorder (SAD). Don't look directly at the sun and don't spend too much time outside unprotected, so you don't get sunburned.

The world around us constantly stimulates our senses by activities beyond our control. It is helpful to reduce irritating or distracting stimulation during the periods we can control.

My Journal

Shower

Find three relaxation techniques that work for you and use them consistently. Deep breathing and alternate nostril breathing should be two of the three. Here's another simple technique. Try it right after you finish reading this segment. Close your eyes and picture yourself in a shower that is the perfect temperature. Feel the water running on your head and neck and shoulders, soothing and relaxing you. Let yourself feel stress flowing out of your body and mind. Enjoy the sensations. See, feel and hear the experience. Involve as many senses as possible, to help ingrain the experience in your mind and body.

An effective way to do this is to actually take a long relaxing shower. While you shower, pay close attention to exactly what it feels like. Remember in detail just how soothing and relaxing it really is. Then, when you are in a stressful situation, it is much easier to recall this pleasant experience. Whenever you visualize like this, remember to also use deep breathing. This is a very strong combination. Our attention and state of relaxation follow our pattern of breathing. We can induce a state of deep relaxation by consciously controlling our breath while we picture or recall a calming situation.

Walking

Finally, take a no pressure walk and enjoy nature and yourself. Calm walks either with someone else or by yourself, can help you relax and maintain perspective. We become so busy, so caught up in current challenges and situations. While you walk, be aware of your surroundings. Be a conscientious listener to those with you, or to the sights and sounds around you. On these walks, leave your cell phone, PDA or iPod, turned off. Let your mind be free from your normal concerns. Be aware of your breathing and allow it to be as calm and slow as possible. Try to feel good about yourself, even if you are in emotional pain. If you are by yourself, attempt to think big, positive thoughts.

> *"He that conceals his grief finds no remedy for it".*
> -- Turkish Proverb
>
> *"Give sorrow words; the grief that does not speak knits up the o'er-wrought heart and bids it break."*
> -- William Shakespeare
>
> Grief and bereavement groups can be wonderfully therapeutic. Consider joining one if you feel that sharing your experiences with others would help.

Allow yourself to drift off for those moments and dream of what the future could hold for you. These walks can rejuvenate and balance you if you will allow them to. And, a calm mind is fertile ground for new ideas, which might be very important as you deal with the loss of your loved one.

Keep a pen and paper in your pocket as you walk, just in case a good idea comes to mind while you walk. Then you can jot it down to remember later, and go back to enjoying your walk.

Your SMART Program

There you have them, the mental and physical techniques you need to begin to remove the causes and effects of stress from your life. Now when you develop a plan for yourself, remember, balance is the key to an effective Stress Management And Relaxation Technique program (SMART). The plan must relieve the symptoms of stress, like tight muscles and feeling rushed, to achieve the much needed temporary relief. It should also work to nullify and remove the deeper causes of stress like poor diet, excess weight, inappropriate behavior patterns, low self-esteem and over scheduling. When you release the causes of stress, the symptoms usually vanish.

Your personal success with managing your stress will depend on several factors. First, write out your plan. In it, include when you are going to exercise and for how long. What time have you set aside each day for your meditation and relaxation practice? Be specific about as many parts of your plan as possible. Then, be consistent. It is better to do something every day for fifteen or twenty minutes than to try and fit all of your stress management activities into one long session. When you try to do too much, it will frustrate you or make the techniques feel like just another chore. Start slowly and keep it simple. Make your plan work for you. Consistency over time is a major key to SMART success.

Don't try to include all the suggestions given in this program into your plan. Try them all, then settle on those two or three in each group that are the easiest and most effective for you. Experiment until you find the right combination. Give yourself permission to pick and choose. You will not like all of the techniques, but you will almost certainly like and benefit from some of them.

If your program begins to feel like a source of stress itself, then try to simplify it even more. Change the order of the techniques that you follow. Change the techniques. Don't let your routines become unconscious

> ### Remember ...
> It is a sign of intelligence and strength, not a sign of weakness, to seek help when needed.

habit. If you do, they will lose their effectiveness. Concentrate when you use the techniques. This way, you will begin to understand how they affect you and how you can gain the most benefits from them.

You must also be honest with yourself. Admit the impact that the loss of your loved one has had on you. Has it been a severe reaction? Did that surprise you? Has it been mild or had almost no impact? Has this surprised you?

Ask yourself if there are any areas in your life that you feel are out of control right now. Are there any areas where professional help or counseling would help you in managing your situation and the resulting stress more effectively? If there are areas where help could make a difference for you, try to find that help.

There are many types of physical and psychological addictions, not just alcohol and drugs. Often they develop as the result of trying to cope with the stress in our life. Smoking and excessive eating habits are often stress related. Trained professionals can help you recognize and overcome the cause of an addiction. They can work with you to prevent a situation from developing into something more serious. Your personal physician, pastor, rabbi, hospice staff, funeral director or trusted friends are possible sources of information to help you get in contact with the proper professionals.

Two final thoughts

1. If you have a good self-image and high self-esteem, you can be successful with your SMART program simply because you like yourself and you want to live a fulfilling life. Because of the death of your loved one, you might not feel that way right now, however, it probably has been your perspective in the past. That is the goal of your SMART program now, to begin to move toward a new normal way of living, adjusted for and impacted by the loss of your loved one.

   You now know that uncontrolled stress is unhealthy and can even be dangerous. If you don't have high self-esteem, begin here. Make this the first and most important part of your personal SMART program. Until you feel good about yourself and know you are worth the effort, it will be difficult to succeed. Dr. Nathaniel

My Journal

Branden is an expert in the field of self-esteem. He has an excellent, seven CD album on the subject titled *The Psychology of High Self Esteem*

2. Like most areas of life, your SMART program is ongoing. It is a good idea to examine and adapt it to your needs regularly; a quarterly review is wise. As you age, your metabolism changes so your dietary needs will change. As your family or business grows or you grow in your line of work and promotions take you to higher levels of responsibility, the type of stress affecting you will change.

No one program will work for everyone. No one specific program will remain effective for you without some periodic changes. The parts of the basic program, Breathing properly, Relaxation techniques, Exercise, Attitude, Diet and Sleep, will stay the same. However, the specific techniques you use should change as your situation changes. It is up to you to develop and maintain an effective personal SMART program that suits you. You are worth it. It should fit your individual needs and personality and also allow you to get the most from your time and efforts.

Now, it is time to develop a plan, to make a personal commitment to follow through with it, and to put your plan into action. You can succeed, and the benefits are worth the effort.

Practical Meditation & Relaxation

In this segment you will learn from the insights and experiences I have had with meditation since I began practicing it daily beginning in 1974. Meditation is an ancient process that is highly effective for relieving stress and balancing brain wave activity. The first written reference to meditation dates back to about 3,000 B.C. and is found in each of the major cultures of the world. This section presents specific, tested methods for calming the mind and increasing the body's state of relaxation. Meditation is a natural process. It is not habit forming and it has no negative side effects. Meditation is neither hypnosis nor auto suggestion. The peak experience of meditation is thoughtless awareness, and it is a natural occurrence within us all. When we remove the stress and distractions inhibiting the mind, we experience the peak as a natural state of mental calmness. During times of extreme stress, like grieving the loss of your loved one, short durations of mental calmness are important to your health.

Everyone can experience the many benefits of proper practice by using the techniques in this section, and by listening to the twenty-minute guided meditation on Session 2 of the attached CD. The benefits are immediate! You can have a positive relaxation experience the first time you meditate. The benefits are also cumulative. Correct daily meditation will lower the habitual level of stress that you experience by lowering your pulse, blood pressure, respiration rate, and expressed fatigue.

You can also experience the benefits of meditation at will. You can meditate in any quiet place, whenever and wherever you like, at any time of the day. And meditation requires no props, support materials or gadgetry.

In the past thirty years, meditation has come out of the realm of religion and into the laboratory to have its claims tested scientifically. And it has held up very well. The most prominent research was done by Dr. Herbert Benson, a cardiologist at Harvard, who called the particular meditation method he studied the "relaxation response." He has written several fine books, which I highly recommend to anyone who wants a

My Journal

scientific explanation for what they experience while meditating. An effective introductory book on the subject is *A Master Guide to Meditation*, by Roy Eugene Davis.

Meditation is a simple procedure that delivers profound results. To those who practice correctly, the effects are obvious, both to themselves and to those around them. Meditation is simple but not always easy. To be successful, one must concentrate without straining. Relax, while remaining fully conscious, and release thoughts and memories without engaging them.

Have an open mind about meditation. Approach it with no preconceptions or firm opinions, during the process. Be the witness of your experiences, not a participant. Don't expect visions or dramatic experiences. Meditation will calm and relax you. It will help you to be a calmer, more productive and balanced person. You will get these results from your regular practice. Also, there is nothing to worry about or fear during meditation. It is a natural process that gives wonderful benefits to both the mind and body.

Five Keys to Successful Meditation

Key #1) Regularity and consistency

Daily meditation, for twenty to thirty minutes is a good starting schedule. Meditating at the same time and in the same conducive environment each day will help reinforce your practice. You will begin to look forward to the experience, making it easier to assume the proper mental set. Be consistent, especially in the beginning. The benefits you receive will convince you to keep meditating. Since it does take some practice to become proficient it is a good idea to be very mindful of how your meditation sessions are going.

Learn to know yourself. Be on the lookout for any "early warning signals" that you are beginning to digress. Times of stress and pressure, like you are experiencing right now, are when meditation will do the most for your balance and well-being. Be consistent and you will reap the rewards.

Key #2) Expect positive results

It is normal to be skeptical about the benefits of meditation. However, it is important to have an open, receptive mind that will allow you to test the claims for yourself. You should believe nothing but direct personal experience. Practice meditation every day for six months, following these guidelines without forming an opinion. Then pass judgment based on your experiences. It is surprising how many people who learn to meditate say, "Wow! It really does work!"

Key #3) Maintain good physical hygiene

This often refers only to sanitary items. However, it includes all aspects of your diet and health. Eat a balanced natural diet; be moderate in your intake of sweets and alcohol. Try to drop caffeine from your diet if it over-stimulates you. Alcohol is a sedative which dulls the mind. It is in direct opposition to the clarity produced by meditation. Good sleep habits and watching what you take in mentally are also helpful. Taking in detrimental material, like disturbing TV shows or movies, will have detrimental results. Everything that goes into our mind remains there. A conscientious person doesn't put "junk food" in their body. You shouldn't put junk into your mind either. This poses the biggest problem when you are mentally weary, confused, depressed or fearful and need the therapeutic benefits of meditation the most. You can help yourself by monitoring what you read and watch.

My Journal

Key #4) Proper posture and a conducive meditation environment

Your posture should be straight and upright, it's very difficult to meditate properly while lying down; we condition our bodies to go to sleep in that position making it hard to meditate effectively. Keep your feet flat on the floor about shoulder-width apart. Place your palms on your thighs. Keep your eyes closed for the duration of your practice. The environment should be quiet, at a comfortable temperature and conducive to relaxation. Also, be sure that the chair you sit in isn't too comfortable. If it is you will tend to slouch, and this causes drowsiness. If you sit up straight, with your back away from the back of the chair, you should have no difficulty remaining alert.

Key #5) Proper meditation practices

There are many meditation techniques. In this section we will go through the major ones. Try each and then settle on what feels the most comfortable for you. Also, recognize your uniqueness and know there is no one technique that is perfect for everyone. Some of us are visual, some auditory, others are kinesthetic (touch oriented).

So, experiment with the various meditation techniques until you find the ones that work well for you.

Then, when you find a technique, or combination of techniques, that you feel good about, stick with them for long enough to experience their positive results. Like anything else, conscientious practice does make perfect. You will reap benefits equal to the quality and consistency of your practice.

And please, be careful not to make your meditation sessions complicated. Don't think that the more techniques you incorporate into your practice, the faster you will progress. That simply isn't true. Don't complicate the process to the point you'd need an outline to tell you what comes next. Just keep it simple. One, possibly two, techniques will be all you need. Some people meditate very effectively by simply watching their breathing pattern.

Common meditation techniques for focusing.

1. Watching your breath,
2. Gazing at your internal light,
3. Listening to your internal sounds,
4. The use of a mantra, which is the mental listening to the repetition of a specific word or phrase, and
5. A combination of two or more of these.

An Example of a Typical Meditation Session

[Session 2 of the attached CD is a twenty-minute guided session.]

Go to your meditation spot at your chosen time. Sit down and close your eyes. Relax, and take two or three long, deep breaths using your stomach and diaphragm, instead of your chest and shoulders. Breathe in relaxation and exhale tension. Internally make a positive statement that this will be a helpful experience. Have the expectation of positive results. Allow your breath to slow and begin to use whatever meditation technique you have chosen. Whatever works the easiest for you will probably be what is most effective for you. Strive for simplicity. No one technique is superior to another.

If your mind wanders, bring it back to your point of focus, your point of concentration, and continue. Some who meditate place their attention on their stomach, others on the tip of their nose if they are watching their breath; others place their attention on the middle of their forehead. Having a point of focus is simply a technique to help you focus your attention and shut out distractions. Don't strain as you focus, be gentle and calm.

My Journal

After a while, your attention will begin to turn outward, and your meditation practice will be over for that session. Sit in the silence, relax for a few moments and picture your life. Feel that the experiences you picture are in tune with your personal destiny. If negative, sad or worrisome thoughts invade your mind while you try to meditate, try to be the observer of the thoughts and breathe calmly until they pass. When you have completed your inner viewing, slowly open your eyes. Try to go about your activities, relaxed and refreshed by your meditation experience.

That's all there is to it. Really!

It is simple and effective, expanding and refreshing. It will help to bring out your healthy, natural qualities.

In summary, be regular with your practice, optimistic in attitude, moderate in your diet and upright in your posture. Meditate correctly, and you will experience positive results. Remember, the techniques you use are points of focus to hang your attention on while your mind calms down. They will naturally fall to the side as your mind becomes still. If your attention ever wanders, just bring it back to your chosen point of focus, and continue. Don't be anxious for results, they will follow proper practice without fail.

Additional Suggestions and Comments

Try to meditate at the same time every day. Then you will begin to look forward to the experience. Once this happens you will find it much easier to calm the mind and breathe. This will help you enter the peak experience faster and remain there longer.

Wear comfortable, loose fitting clothing that will not bind or restrict you. Levi's had a humorous commercial that emphasized this point. It said: *"Forget cholesterol, it's the jeans cutting off circulation!"*

Choose a quiet, conducive atmosphere to meditate in. Either

turn off your phone and cell phone, or ask someone else in the house to take calls for you while you meditate.

Keep your meditation practice and experiences to yourself. If friends want to know about meditation, let them read this section of the Guide & Journal or let them listen to Session 2 of the attached CD. Be careful not to allow your practice to become disruptive to your home environment. Meditation is to calm and harmonize, not disrupt. You should be able to find a way to meditate privately.

Maintain an erect, comfortable posture. Hold your head upright. If you are sitting in a chair, keep your feet flat on the floor, shoulder width apart; do not cross your legs. Keep your hands on your thighs, either palm up or down, whichever is most comfortable for you.

Give whatever technique you decide to use a six-month test. This will allow you to become familiar and comfortable with it. Your body will become accustomed to the technique and will respond positively each time you use it. Jumping from technique to technique will complicate the process and slow your progress.

Don't meditate immediately after eating. Try to allow at least an hour between meals and meditating, two hours if possible. Meditation and digestion are opposite processes.

A few minutes of light, gentle stretching before you begin to meditate will make it easier to sit still. It will also help calm your mind and breath and release some of the stiffness in your body.

After the peak experience for a given meditation session, you will naturally begin to regain body awareness and thoughts will start to stir. This is a unique time. A calm mind and relaxed body provide the perfect opportunity to work on creative imagination. The left and right hemispheres of the brain are more in balance, and the door to the

My Journal

subconscious is easily accessible. Picture and feel your challenges as already resolved and your goals as already attained. See and feel yourself as being happy, healthy and in tune with life around you. Given the death of your loved one, this might be hard. However, this technique is an effective way to help break the grasp that negativity and depression might have on your mind and emotions.

Feel open to ideas and insight. Then, after your meditation session is over, go about your day allowing the feeling of meditation to remain with you as much and as long as you can.

[Please pay close attention to this next suggestion; this is a major point. If you can grasp the significance of this, you can effectively control many aspects of your life.]

There is a definite correlation and connection between the activity of the mind and the breath. When you are calm-minded you breathe in a relaxed rhythmic way. When excited, you breathe rapidly and might even hyperventilate. The key to this information is that you can reverse the process. If you begin to breathe slower and deeper than normal, using your diaphragm, it will have an immediate calming effect on the mind. The body may initially continue

CD Session 2

Session 2 of the attached CD is a twenty-minute guided meditation session. While listening to it, you will use several different meditation techniques - each of them works alone or in combination with other techniques.

Find what works for you and then stick with it. Keep the process simple. After experimenting, tailor a meditation session that fits you. The guided meditation is by no means the only way for you to approach meditation. It is an effective, result-producing method, but not the only way.

to race for a moment or two. However, if you persist in gently controlling your breath, calmness will occur. This will allow you to calm the mind and enter true meditation faster. Don't hold your breath, or breathe too hard. Just gently coax yourself towards a calmer, slower breathing pattern using your stomach and diaphragm instead of your chest and shoulders.

Not all meditation sessions will be equally productive. Some sessions will be more effective than others. There are three distinct levels of meditation experience: basic, maintenance and mastery.

1. **Basic meditation** is practiced to release the symptoms of stress like lowering the blood pressure, and pulse. It is also useful in gaining relief from the subjective feelings of internal rushing or emotional "burn out." These benefits are important. However, there is more to meditation than relaxation and focusing. Sometimes the relaxation is so complete many people stop there, believing that this is meditation. If you will be consistent and patient with your practice, you will experience much beyond relaxation.

2. **Maintenance Meditation** occurs when you are successful in your practice and are now meditating to enhance and maintain the benefits you experience. However, you have not yet begun to use meditation to increase your intellect and self-awareness.

3. **Mastery Meditation** and its profound benefits come to the dedicated, serious practitioner. Creativity increases, and you experience personal serenity and a greater overall perspective about life.

Besides these three stages of meditation that you will experience over time, you will probably find

My Journal

there is a qualitative difference between your morning and evening practices. This is due to the differing mind-sets you have when you begin each meditation session.

Just as a newly planted seed will not grow if you dig it up each day to see how it's doing, your meditations will suffer from continual comparisons. Relax about your practice. Be diligent, and allow yourself the opportunity to become accustomed to your specific technique. Be gentle with yourself. Meditation is something productive that you are doing. Don't be too analytical about it either. Just let time go by and you will notice the benefits occurring naturally.

And finally,

Probably the single most important point to remember is: **Meditation is not a process that makes something happen.** You are actually allowing the mind to stop thinking, thereby calming itself. You are allowing your breathing pattern to slow, which in turn increases the level of relaxation you experience. A calm mind and slow breathing relax the body. Relaxation releases stress, lowers the pulse and blood pressure and eases muscular tension. The peak experience of meditation is "thought-free awareness" experienced by a calm mind in a highly relaxed body that is breathing at a very low rate because of reduced oxygen demands.

Stress affects many people making them depressed or irritable and habitually tired or unable to sleep. Some say that they do not meditate because they are too tired. More accurately, it might be that they are too tired because they did not meditate. Allow yourself to give meditation a *bona fide*, six-month place in your daily life and then, you be the judge. You decide for yourself whether or not meditation is right for you.

An Overview of Sleep

Each of us spends about one-third of our life in bed. Yet many of us aren't getting the maximum benefits from what should be a time of rest and rejuvenation.

Many have at least occasional problems sleeping. For most people *The Sleep Technique* (Session 3 of the attached CD) will bring immediate relief, while others may require medical help. By the end of this section, you should know which group you fit into.

This overview will give you an understanding of what is going on inside while you are sleeping. Up until 1935, researchers believed sleep to be a simple, passive and uniform state. Now it is known to be active and complex with separate and distinctive brain wave patterns. 1953 actually marked the beginning of modern sleep research with the discovery of Rapid Eye Movements, commonly called REM. Much of the mystery that once surrounded sleep no longer exists. It has been unveiled through scientific research. By paying attention to what these researchers have found, you can learn to sleep better.

Science now knows that there are two types and four stages of sleep called "Sleep Architecture" by professionals. These stages and types of sleep merge and overlap. Researchers identify them by their distinct brain wave patterns.

The two types of sleep are dream sleep and non-dream sleep. They alternately occur at or about ninety-minute intervals in adults and about sixty-minute intervals in children. Technically, they are REM sleep because of the presence of rapid eye movements during dreams and NON-REM sleep because of the absence of eye movements during the non-dreaming stage of sleep.

My Journal

Regarding sleep, there are seven or eight recurring questions people often ask.

I never dream, is there something wrong?

Truth is, everyone dreams. Although some people say that they never dream, we all have three to six dream sleep episodes each night and each episode involves dreaming. We simply forget the dreams that we have unless we awaken in them and consciously think about them. Most likely, those who say they never dream are less interested in their inner life and have fewer dream awakenings.

Does everyone dream the same?

No. Several studies show that we have basically the same personality in our dreams that we have when we're awake. Creative types have more creative dreams, while psychotics have bizarre, fragmented ones. Research also suggests there is a pattern to each person's dream content. Dreams that we have early in the night are often a simple replay of current activities, while later dreams are more complex and likely to be unusual.

I wake up at 5:00 a.m. ready to go but others in the house drag around until 10:00 a.m. and then are up all night. Why is that?

This is due to the interaction of various "circadian rhythms." This term commonly refers to the alternating cycles of sleep and wakefulness. It is about twenty-five hours long in humans. Researchers have found that we have cues that we respond to that help us orient ourselves and stay on schedule. Clocks, mealtimes, work hours, and sunlight are all recurring cues. A regular and consistent waking time is probably the strongest sleep cue of all.

Other circadian rhythms, such as sleep, body temperature, and metabolism, account for some people

---

Dream & Non-dream Sleep

The mind is very active during dream sleep. The heart rate and neurological firings in various portions of the brain suggest that dream sleep is as active mentally as wakefulness.

Some researchers feel that the function of sleep is physical rest during non-dream sleep and assimilation of information during dream sleep.

---

being "early risers" and others being "night owls." The difference depends on when their systems peak during the day.

What is the right number of hours of sleep for someone?

There is a range, researchers have found, to what is normal. The norm is around seven to eight hours per night in a healthy adult. Most people fall within this range. However, there are "long sleepers and short sleepers." The range is about seven and one-half to nine hours for the long sleepers and five and one-half to seven hours for the short sleepers. Dr. Ernest Hartmann's research suggests that introverted, sensitive people sleep longer, while the short sleeper is more outgoing and ambitious. It is good to be sensitive to ourselves and our sleep needs and just try to get enough sleep. "Enough sleep" is basically the amount that a healthy individual needs to wake up refreshed. Please realize also, sleep requirements can vary within a single individual in relationship to stress, diet, and exercise habits. The well-conditioned person requires less sleep. The over-stressed person requires more. During times of grief and mourning, restful sleep is often more difficult and it then takes more hours in bed to get enough sleep.

My Journal

I've missed a full night's sleep. Will it take me days to catch up?

It shouldn't. A useful and interesting fact is that it does not take an equal amount of time to "catch-up" lost or missed sleep. Usually, after two nights of regular sleep most people are back to normal.

I used to need eight full hours of sleep when I was working. Now I am retired and can't sleep that long though I have all the time in world.

This is because the length of required sleep usually decreases with age. The length of required sleep is highest in newborns, seventeen hours. Four-year olds require ten to twelve hours, while ten-year olds need nine to ten hours of sleep. At puberty sleep needs quickly drop to seven and one-half to eight hours staying level until the late fifties, with a decrease to about six and one-half hours in the elderly.

I work nights and always feel out of synch with my family.

When there are frequent changes in the daily routine every few weeks or so, the internal clock does not have enough time to reset. Permanent night shift workers sometimes have difficulties on their days off when they try to adjust to the daylight routines of their families and friends. "Jetlag" is a

Sleep Disorders

There are individuals who have very real physiological or psychological problems that affect their sleep.

If you think that the cause of your sleeping difficulty is one of the disorders that I am about to discuss, know there is help available and contact your regular physician and ask for a referral to a sleep specialist. Or, call a neurologist in your area.

Not all sleep problems are "in your head." Some have very real causes and require medical treatment.

similar sleep/wake cycle disorder. Our circadian rhythm gets out of step by crossing time zones and we need to reset our internal clocks.

Good sleepers are less affected by different types of disruption than are poor sleepers. And younger sleepers are more flexible about changes in schedules than older sleepers.

If you are only going to be off schedule for a few days, you will probably adjust quickly to your normal routine. However, if the disruption is for a prolonged period, and you have difficulty re-acclimating to your regular environment, you might need to seek professional help in resetting your internal clock. It might sound odd, but it can be a serious problem.

Three Main Groups of Physiological Sleep Disorders

During your bereavement, you might experience any or all of the three types of sleep disorders. However, it should be a temporary condition and *The Sleep Technique* (Session 3 of the attached CD) should help you through this difficult time.

Group #1: Insomniacs

These are people who have problems falling or remaining asleep. This is the most common complaint of persons visiting a sleep clinic. The eight keys to good sleep I will discuss below and *The Sleep Technique* (Session 3 of at attached CD) are mainly for this group.

Group #2: People who sleep too much

Narcolepsy is the most famous disorder in this group. This is the opposite of insomnia. Society is not as sympathetic to those who sleep too much as they are to insomniacs. We often think of people who complain of falling asleep as being lazy. Because of this lack of acceptance, the size of this group is difficult to determine.

My Journal

Group #3: People who have problems during their sleep

These problems occur only during sleep or sleep exaggerates them. They include bedwetting, sleep walking, teeth grinding, breathing problems, seizures, and nightmares. And an unusual problem called sleep paralysis where the person afflicted is awake and aware but unable to move their body.

If, over time, you have difficulty sleeping and *The Sleep Technique* is not effective in relieving your problem, then ask yourself the following questions. Your answer might reveal the cause of your problem.

Question #1: Could my sleep problem be due to an alcohol or drug addiction?

Even prescription drugs can be a problem if taken incorrectly or for an extended time.

Question #2: Why do I wake up during the night gasping for breath?

Sleep apnea, or sleep-induced breathing problems, can be fatal. Often, this is a problem with the windpipe or jaw. When treated or repaired, normal sleep usually returns.

Question #3: Why do I snore so much that it wakes me up (or keeps others awake)?

This is a problem in the same group as stated previously. It is a disorder of maintaining sleep. Like other breathing problems, something can usually be done to correct the situation.

Question #4: Does it take me an excessive length of time to fall asleep? Does this mean I'm a poor sleeper?

Sleep researchers define poor sleep as being asleep less than eighty percent of the time in bed. During an eight-hour night of sleep, that would mean being awake for more than one and one-half hours. Many factors can cause us to take a long time to fall asleep, like stress, diet, worry or caffeine. The eight keys to good sleep and *The Sleep Technique* will both help you improve your ability to fall asleep.

Some sleep problems are temporary. Times of grief or unusual stress can also cause a temporary

> **Remember . . .**
> Good sleep is an important requirement for your mental, physical and emotional health.

sleep disorder. We all have this type of trouble periodically. ***The Sleep Technique*** will be especially useful to you during these occasions.

There are both mental and physical causes of sleep disorders and very often both are present. If five to seven nights of open-minded use of ***The Sleep Technique*** doesn't help and you are following all the major suggestions outlined in the next section, then make an appointment with a medical sleep therapist or a sleep psychologist to determine the nature and extent of what your sleep problem is. Also, there are, professionally staffed, sleep disorder centers where you can have your sleep analyzed.

The Eight Keys to Good Sleep

This section offers specific guidelines for getting the greatest benefit from using ***The Sleep Technique***, thereby increasing its worth to you so you will fall asleep easily and experience more restful and refreshing sleep.

Strong, sleep habits are also effective time management tools. Most of us spend one-third of our life in bed. If we enhance the quality of that time, we also improve the

My Journal

effectiveness of our waking hours. We function better when we sleep better.

There are eight steps to good sleep, which I term the eight sleep keys. Each will improve your ability to sleep. Follow as many of these keys as possible.

Key # 1: Sleep Naturally

Avoid sleeping pills unless completely necessary and then use them only for a short period and under strict medical supervision. Drugs relieve symptoms and seldom affect causes. Drugs and alcohol can induce sleep, but only disturbed and fragmented sleep. They can actually make you a "problem sleeper." Nicotine is a potent stimulant. Heavy smokers are often poor sleepers. Once people stop smoking, their sleep will usually improve.

Key #2: Diet

Eating habits can strongly affect the quality of your sleep. Cut back on sugar intake. Drop caffeine if practical. If you drink coffee or tea, try the decaffeinated varieties. Chocolate and cola drinks also contain caffeine. If you decide to continue your caffeine intake, restrict it to the morning. Eat lightly at the evening meal, at least two hours before retiring. If you feel hungry at bedtime, eat a light snack. Some research suggests that a snack

of cheese and crackers, or other protein/carbohydrate combination, is most helpful. If you have a dairy allergy, it would be better for you to find a different bedtime snack.

Key #3: Exercise

This improves conditioning and lowers stress. Try to exercise in the morning, afternoon or early evening. Avoid hard exercise just before bedtime. Your body requires time to slow down after the stimulation of exercise. Light stretching just before bedtime is helpful. It will remove the stiffness of the day and make it possible to lie in bed for longer.

> *"Courage is being afraid and going on the journey anyhow".*
> *-- John Wayne*
>
> *The journey of a thousand miles begins with the first step"*
> *-- Chinese Proverb*
>
> Grief is a journey that requires no physical travel, however, it can be the most exhausting journey you ever undertake. Sleep and rest might be difficult right now, but still try. Use these techniques and suggestions, they will help you.

Key #4: Read Inspirational Material

Read a page or two of inspirational material at bedtime. As words that offer hope make us feel better, reading about the significant accomplishments and heroic deeds of others inspires us. Read the material on a regular, nightly basis. Be flexible also, a page or two some nights, a paragraph another. Enjoy the reading; allow it to be relaxing and uplifting. Read inspirational non-fiction at bedtime; do your mystery/suspense reading during the day or early evening. This goes double for television, the internet, email, texting, or video games. The goal is relaxation and some writers and activities are so realistic that you will be "wound up" instead of relaxed.

Key #5: Keep A Notebook

This is important! Keep a notebook, pen and a small flashlight on your nightstand. After you have read your inspirational material, review the day and then think about tomorrow. Is there anything that you forgot to do today? Are there any notes about tomorrow to make, any appointments to remember? Don't feel compelled to come up with something to write down. Just list what you want to let go of until morning. If you had any sad, challenging or unpleasant experiences during the day, did you

My Journal

handle them well? If not, write out a solution. If you need to, review, revise and release the situation. Do it now either mentally or in the notebook or the journal portion of this book. This way you can sleep, knowing that you have made every effort to be thorough in your remembering and planning. If you wake up during the night with something on your mind, write it down (use the little flashlight instead of a full room light). By writing thoughts and ideas in your notebook, you won't feel the need to try to remember them until morning. You can now roll over and go back to sleep.

Key #6: Attitude

Studies have shown that we have a tendency to grow into whatever we believe to be true about ourselves. Our self-image and self-picture become the blueprint for a self-fulfilling prophecy. If your feelings about sleep are positive, if you can believe that falling asleep easily and sleeping well are possible for you. Then you will increase the opportunity to experience these results.

Use affirmations & visualizations. By repeating positive statements to yourself you can begin to alter your attitude and underlying beliefs. The body responds positively to praise, regardless of who gives it. Tell yourself that you are happy and relaxed, one

of the fortunate few who always sleep well. Then live the reality of the statement. Use gentle visualization to see yourself in an environment conducive to sleeping well. See yourself in a hammock on an island. Feel yourself floating on a raft, and drifting off to sleep.

Key #7: Use Relaxation Tools

This will help you make the change from your work day mentality to your sleeping mode. There are two main tools: correct breathing and meditation.

The first tool is correct breathing. Increasing the depth and

CD Session 3

The Sleep Technique (Session 3 of the attached CD) is highly effective. The procedure should be listened to several times, paying close attention to its sequence.

Then try to go through it by yourself. Just recall the instructions and guide yourself through the process.

Once you can follow the technique you will have mastered your ability to go to sleep. Then you can sleep wherever you are, whenever you need to.

slowing the rate of breathing will relax and calm you. There is a connection between mental activity and the rate of breathing. Slow = calm, fast = active. Be conscious of your breath at bedtime and slowly begin to breathe slightly deeper and longer than normal. Don't hold your breath just smoothly breathe in and out. Use your diaphragm for this deeper breathing; allow your chest and shoulders to rest.

The second tool is meditation. As you learned earlier in this book, meditation is a highly effective way to relax anytime, anywhere. It is a procedure for stopping the thinking process and resting in a conscious state of relaxed awareness. Correct meditation and experiencing stress cannot exist simultaneously. In the beginning, use Session 2 of the attached CD to guide your meditation sessions.

Key #8: Observe your thoughts at bedtime

You probably have a set pattern of behavior at bedtime. You brush your teeth, wash your face or take a shower. You put on pajamas and lay out clothes for the next day. It is a routine you have repeated for so long, you no longer pay much attention to it. What do you think about while preparing for bed? What internal conversations do you carry on?

My Journal

When you decide to go to sleep, think positively about the experience. Remind yourself how relaxed you will be soon, how refreshed you will feel after a good night's sleep. Be conscious of each activity that you perform in preparation for lying down. Think only about getting ready to go to sleep. Begin to slow your breathing as you brush your teeth and put on your pajamas. You will have time to remember whatever you need to when you get to your notebook. After a few nights of restful sleep, this routine will become self-fulfilling because of the positive reinforcement of sleeping well.

These keys will help you as much as you will allow them to. Keep a high level of enthusiasm about your ability to learn to sleep well. It might take several days for the positive effects of some of the changes you make to become clear. The Sleep Technique will help you right away. Tonight you should fall asleep within twenty minutes. Follow the instructions. They are clear and easy. Relax about the whole process of sleeping. It is a natural event that will occur when you release any obstructions inhibiting you.

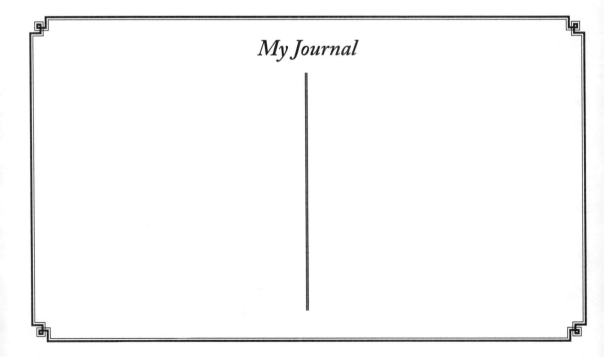

My Journal

My Journal

"When someone you love becomes a memory,
the memory becomes a treasure. "
--Author Unknown

Compassion Fatigue:
"Who takes care of the caretakers?"

[This is a full explanation of the condition briefly mentioned earlier in the Guide on page 11.]

When you are constantly exposed to and involved with the environment of grief and loss, with others either asking for or expecting your support and guidance to get through your mutual loss, you might experience an additional level of mental, emotional, and physical symptoms of sickness, depression and psychological instability.

Thanks to the work of psychologists like Martin Seligman, Karen Reivich, Andrew Shatte and others, there are now specific approaches to dealing with the extra stress of being a major source of support and guidance to others who are grieving, while you grieve yourself.

These researchers have built on the early post-traumatic stress disorder (PTSD) work by Dr. Charles Figley and Martin Seligman's *Learned Optimism*. And, they have substantiated the BREADS Formula approach first developed in 1989 and expanded in 2000 and 2009.

Dealing with the finality of death, the ultimate human stressor, is hard enough by itself. When you add in the extra burden of being the source of strength or support for others, it can become even more overwhelming.

Without some specific sources of at least temporary relief, like regular personal time, and good dietary, sleep and exercise habits, it is likely that you will experience occasional episodes of what psychologist Charles Figley calls compassion fatigue. These episodes will vary in frequency, intensity and duration. However, even mild events can have significant consequences and add extra stress to your already overloaded systems.

Dr. Figley is a professor of psychology at Tulane University in New Orleans. He is an internationally recognized expert on Post-Traumatic Stress Disorder (PTSD). Dr. Figley found in his research another class of stress disorder, secondary traumatic stress. In a situation involving the death of a loved one, the traumatic stress experience was the ultimate one, the death of your loved one. The secondary sufferers are the survivors. So, all grieving survivors of the lost loved one experience a degree of this secondary stress because of the overwhelming nature of the experience.

Compassion fatigue is an even more severe secondary traumatic stress experience caused by your involvement with the people to whom you provide support and guidance. It is almost like you get a double dose of stress, which is further exacerbated by the other demands made on you to run a successful practice, business, household or life outside of your personal mourning.

While it is easier to recognize than solve these problems, you can exert more control than you might currently believe. The solution is similar

> *"There is no grief like the grief that does not speak"*
> *– Henry Wadsworth Longfellow*
>
> Private grief counselors, therapists and members of the clergy can all help you talk about your grief and mourning experiences.
> Sometimes friends are not enough or a group setting does not fit a person's personality. These are the times to consider and to use private help.

to the one you would use to manage your grief. Developing a personal **S**tress **M**anagement **A**nd **R**elaxation **T**echnique **(SMART)** program will give you the tools to take care of you, your family and others you are helping during this time of loss. Remember, any situation that subjects you to continuous, unrelenting stress can trigger a compassion fatigue episode and requires an effective process for relief.

The main problem is that severe or continuous stress causes disruptions in sleep and dietary patterns further weakening already highly taxed immune and psychological systems. When devising your personal SMART

Program, you need to consider the three parts of the stress/grief/mourning cycle that we discussed previously: frequency, intensity and duration.

Your personal program, for dealing effectively with compassion fatigue has twelve parts. This is an expanded version of the six-part BREADS formula presented earlier for those in mourning. The difference for those of you who also suffer from compassion fatigue is you must to be even more vigilant about your mental, physical and emotional health because you have additional, unique challenges that others don't.

The additional six steps in this expanded version of BREADS build on the first six. One or two of the parts might seem insensitive; they are not intended to. Each part deals directly with one of the increased challenges that you face as a person who is both grieving and turned to by others for comfort or help.

As I've cautioned earlier, do not try to implement all twelve of these ideas and techniques at once. The goal is to reduce your stress. Read through the following steps, selecting the one or two that you believe you can incorporate into your life right now. Use what you already do well as your foundation and gently build up your program over time.

My Journal

The twelve-part BREADS formula

1. **Breathe** correctly using your diaphragm to relax or your chest when you need to feel energized.
2. **Believe** in something greater than yourself.
3. Practicing **Relaxation** techniques daily, like meditation or hatha yoga.
4. Develop and maintain strong close **Relationships**.
5. **Exercise** aerobically three or four times per week for thirty or more minutes. Be sure to get a physical before starting any new exercise program. Walking is a great way to begin to include exercise in your daily routine.
6. **Educate** yourself more about stress management. *The Resilience Factor* by Reivich and Shatte is an excellent book to consider.
7. Monitor your **Attitude**. Try to keep it positive and forward looking. That is sometimes very difficult, even temporarily impossible, while you mourn. Reading a book or other source of solace and inspiration often helps. Take a break when you find your attitude ruminating and becoming negative. If your dealings with others you help during this difficult time have a strong impact on you, be sure to get some quiet personal time to think and collect your thoughts.
8. Keep **Active**. Have a hobby. Bird watch, fish, hike, garden, volunteer or get out in nature; these can all be very therapeutic.
9. Eat a healthy balanced **Diet**. As part of your education, learn about proper nutrition, it is very important. You can eat well and still enjoy what you eat.
10. **Determination** is the next step. Resolve to be resilient. Work to develop what psychologists call a "hardy personality." Following the twelve steps of this expanded **BREADS** formula can help you become strong and hardy. This does not mean you should become uncaring or insensitive. It does mean you can, over time, develop a more resilient way of living.
11. **Sleep** naturally and get at least six hours of restful sleep per night. This is nature's number one restorative power. *The Sleep Technique,* on the attached CD will help you.
12. Develop **Serenity**, the sense of inner calmness that comes from accepting life as good and death as the common end for all of us. Time allows for a change of perspective to occur. With this change can come a better understanding and acceptance of the totality of experiences we call our life.

My Journal

"Blessed are those who mourn, for they shall be comforted."
-- Jesus Christ, Matthew 5:4

"Do not protect yourself from grief by a fence,
but rather by your friends."
-- Czech Proverb

Bereavement & Grief Groups

Here is information about where to find help in your area, what to expect and what to look for if you decide to join a grief or bereavement group or seek the help of a counselor or therapist. These ideas and suggestions are a starting point in your search for help not a complete list. However, you will find some of the major groups involved in the bereavement area.

Your funeral director, clergy person, local hospice and mental health agencies are also good resources for direction and help.

Characteristics, Benefits, & Resources

Choosing a group that is a good fit for you can feel challenging. Here are a few characteristics that effective groups seem to have in common.

- They are led by a formally trained person.
- They have an accepting environment where participants feel welcomed, comfortable and unthreatened (although the first meeting might make you feel uneasy because it is new. Give the group a chance).
- The leader and other group members are good listeners.

You will have ample opportunity to express yourself and what you are feeling. It is important for you to be a good listener also for two main reasons. First, listening is how you will get ideas, feedback and learn. Second, it is kind to listen to those who have patiently listened to you.

- They are made up of peers; people who have experienced the same or very similar loss that you have. Often, there are groups for those who have lost a spouse, or a child or a sibling. By being in a group of peers, there is a better chance of mutual understanding.
- They offer a sense of hope, comfort and support.

Remember, joining or not joining a group is your decision. You should not feel obligated. If you feel confused or indecisive about groups, ask a trusted friend, member of the clergy or your Funeral Director to help you think it through.

Benefits of A Bereavement Group

Each person has different experiences in a group setting. And each of us goes into a group experience with different expectations. Here are some commonly expressed benefits that group participants have said they experienced.

- Mental and emotional support and understanding in a comfortable, non-judgmental setting.
- Insights from others on how they are dealing with their loss which might give you some understanding about your own feelings and challenges, one reason why it is important to be a good listener.
- The opportunity to learn effective coping skills to help you with your most difficult and persistent grief episodes.
- The realization that you are not alone. There are others who have suffered a similar loss and who are also looking for answers, help and guidance.
- Time: time to let the bereavement process follow its natural progression for you. Time to be off, and away,

from your normal routine. Time for you to be with others outside your family, friends and associates.

- An increased sense of hope. As you watch others progress toward their new normal life, you will eventually begin to see yourself progressing toward your new normal life as well.

Resources to Find a Bereavement Group, Counselor or Therapist in Your Area.

If your funeral director, clergy person or friends are either not available or have no suggestions, your local hospice, because of federally mandated requirements to offer certain bereavement counseling services, is a good place to start if you want to find a bereavement group or counseling.

There are many good groups and resources. Here are some that I have found useful both personally and professionally.

All of these resources listed below, and their web site links are also available to you at:

www.griefguideandjournal.com/griefresources

————

The National Hospice and Palliative Care Organization contains a directory of local support groups and organizations.

www.nhpco.org

From their website:

"The National Hospice and Palliative Care Organization (NHPCO) is the oldest and largest nonprofit membership organization representing hospice and palliative care programs and professionals in the United States. The organization is committed to improving end-of-life care and expanding access to hospice care with the goal of profoundly enhancing quality of life for people dying in America and their loved ones."

————

National Hospice Foundation
www.nationalhospicefoundation.org
From their website:
"We are the National Hospice Foundation--committed to compassionate care at the end of life. We envision a world where everyone facing serious illness, death, and grief will experience the best that humankind can offer."

———

Hospice Foundation of America has a list of local groups.
www.hospicefoundation.org
From their website:
"We recommend using your local hospice as a resource. Under the Medicare Hospice Benefit, hospices provide bereavement counseling for at least a year to families of patients they have served. They also provide counseling to partners and close friends. Often, hospices provide this support to people in their community even if the death did not occur with hospice care."

———

The National Funeral Directors Association has an area on their web site for the public entitled "Grief Resources." One section, "Grief-related Information and Organizations," allows you to search for services available in your area.
www.nfda.org

———

International Cemetery, Cremation and Funeral Association
http://consumer.iccfa.com/
From their website:
Straight answers to real questions about funeral and cemetery arrangements, cremation, grief and other issues related to the end of life. No family should have to face the loss of a loved one uninformed and unprepared.

———

Good Grief Center's "Good Help, 20 Tips" written by Mark D. Miller, M.D. These "20 tips," are profound insights that will help you in dealing with your loss.
www.goodgriefcenter.com/help/twenty_tips.php

———

Good Grief and Good Grief Groups This group has workshops based on the book *Good Grief*, by Granger Westbrook and uses workbook materials by Cecil Fike.

www.goodgriefgroups.com

From their website:

"The goal of Good Grief Groups is to create an atmosphere in hospitals, churches, funeral homes, and other organizations in which those who grieve can find healing. This is accomplished through mutual support, sharing, and understanding from other members of the group, along with the materials presented in the workbook."

Here is how Good Grief answered a question about Grief/Bereavement Groups:

"I've never been to a support group. What are they like?

Support groups are made up of individuals who are seeking an accepting environment with empathic listeners who are supportive and non-judgmental. A support group should offer comfort and hope. Good Grief Center has an extensive listing of support groups, so contact us to find one that might be right for you. support@goodgriefcenter.com"

———

Compassionate Friends This is a non-profit nationwide network offering support for bereaved parents and siblings after the death of a child.

www.compassionatefriends.org

From their website:

"The Compassionate Friends is about transforming the pain of grief into the elixir of hope. It takes people out of the isolation society imposes on the bereaved and lets them express their grief naturally. With the shedding of tears, healing comes. And the newly bereaved get to see people who have survived and are learning to live and love again."

—Simon Stephens, founder of The Compassionate Friends

———

AARP This group was originally called "The American Association for Retired People," however as they expanded their services and activities, they changed their name to just "AARP." They provide information and resources for surviving spouses.

www.aarp.org/family/lifeafterloss

———

The American Foundation for Suicide Prevention This is an organization that offers support for those whose loved one committed suicide.

www.afsp.org

———

The Association for Death Education and Counseling has a database of professionals who are trained to work with the bereaved.

www.adec.org

———

GriefNet is a companion site to the KidsAid website mentioned below.

www.griefnet.org

From their website:

"GriefNet.org is an Internet community of persons dealing with grief, death, and major loss. We have almost 50 e-mail support groups and two web sites. Our integrated approach to on-line grief support provides help to people working through loss and grief issues of many kinds."

———

KidsAid is a companion site to GriefNet.

www.kidsaid.com

From their website:

". . . provides a safe environment for kids and their parents to find information and ask questions. It is a safe place for kids to help each other deal with grief and loss. It's a place to deal with feelings in our e-mail support group, to share and view artwork and stories, and for parents and kids to ask questions and find answers."

———

National Directory of Hospice Palliative Care Services for Canada

www.oulton.com/chpca

From their website:

"Welcome to the Canadian Directory of Hospice Palliative Care Services. This on-line directory has been designed to provide you with information on the availability of hospice palliative care services across Canada. Here you will find a listing of programs and services, their contact information, the population they serve, and where they provide care."

————

Hello Grief has a State-by-State resource listing of groups and services available. I found them helpful personally because they confront the cultural indifference about grief and mourning that is pervasive in the United States.

www.hellogrief.org

From their website:

" We're not afraid to talk about GRIEF and LOSS. Hello Grief provides information and resources about grief in order to break through the current culture of avoidance that surrounds death and loss. Instead, Hello Grief addresses bereavement head-on for those who are helping others cope, as well as those who need support on their own personal journey with grief. In a world that doesn't get it, we do."

————

This is not an exhaustive list of resources. However, it is a good list to help you move in a positive direction toward finding the resources and help that is available to you and your family, both in your area and on the Internet. Please consider using some of these resources; they and the people behind them are there to help you deal with the loss of your loved one.

Again, all of these resources that I have listed, and their web site links are also available to you at:

www.griefguideandjournal.com/griefresources

"And can it be that in a world so full and busy the loss of one person makes a void so wide and deep that nothing but the width and depth of eternity can fill it up?"
-- Charles Dickens

Final Thoughts: Saying Goodbye

4/26/2010

This program is for you. The hope is that you will find some comfort and solace from it during this time of adjustment to a new way of living without the loved one you have lost to death.

Today as I conclude my writing, it is my birthday, and I am in tears as I type knowing that my mom and dad won't call me today to sing *"Happy Birthday Timbo!"* They can't, they are gone. It has been eight years since they last called. Dad died six years ago and for the last two years of his life he couldn't easily get on the phone. I can hear them singing though, and the tears are now as much tears of gratitude and joy as they are tears of sorrow. I am grateful they were my parents. Thankful for the example they set, the morals they instilled, the generosity they so freely exhibited and the sense of humor we all enjoyed as a family. Writing that just now was healing for me. And once again, I say goodbye and thank you to them and I'm smiling, the joy of all the good I remember, now outweighs any sadness.

Time does heal, to a point. You will likely, eventually, begin to live what you will consider a normal life again. It might include much of your former life and surroundings, or it could be a whole new beginning. Don't force a timeline on your grieving. Literally try to live each day the best you can. There will be dark nights, long days, wondering, wishing, hoping, confusion and despair. Use the techniques and ideas in this guide to help you deal with and work through those episodes. Use the journal to remember, to plan, to wonder and hope.

I believe there will be for you, a day like there was for me, when I noticed a subtle change. Quietly, slowly, but definitely, hope began to move in me again. I found myself having longer periods of acceptance without the intense denial and questioning.

When this day arrives for you, whenever it is, you will then know that you are beginning to leave the Season for Healing and are realizing there is a Reason for Hope. Be gentle with yourself, you deserve it.

Sincerely,

Timothy J. O'Brien
Tallahassee, Florida

About the Author

Timothy J. O'Brien, M.S. is the Director of The Institute for Stress Management & Performance Improvement, in Tallahassee, Florida. He is a Fellow of the American Institute of Stress and a Life Member of the International Society for Performance Improvement.

He has presented at both Florida Funeral Directors Association (FFDA) & National Funeral Directors Association (NFDA) Conventions and has authored several articles for their magazines including the cover story for the NFDA's official magazine; "The Director" (vol. 82 -1).

Tim is the author of the popular continuing education course *Grief Management: The Role of the Funeral Service Practitioner,* offered by the NFDA. For 14 years, he wrote a column for Knight Ridder Tribune News Service and has published more than 400 articles and given presentations on grief, compassion fatigue, stress and performance improvement.

My Journal

Index

PILL BOTTLE SCENT CONTAINER

To keep scent where a deer can smell it, try combining a pill bottle and a clothespin. Use camouflage tape to attach a pill bottle to a clothespin. You can use cotton to hold the scent, but I think a sponge works better. Cut strips to use inside the bottle.

You can place this device along trails or around your stand. Fox urine works great as a cover scent. Use doe-in-heat scent during the rut. When you move to a new stand, just pop the top on the bottle and take it to the next location, where you can clip it to a twig or small tree branch and pop the top off!

Carry the pill bottle/clothespin scent container in a zip-top bag in case the top comes off.

Kenny Crummett
Sugar Grove, West Virginia

A clothespin, pill bottle and camouflage tape takes scent dispersal to new heights.

MAKE ANTLER BUTTONS

To keep my gun sling comfortably on my shoulder, I sew an antler "button" onto the shoulder of my coat. Here's what to do:

Take a whitetail's antler and slice it on a bandsaw $\frac{3}{16}$-inch thick and $1\frac{1}{4}$-inch in diameter. Drill four $\frac{1}{32}$-inch holes into the center so it resembles a button. Find the spot on your coat's shoulder where the gun sling rests comfortably and sew the antler button just below that spot. The antler button acts as a stopper to prevent your rifle sling, bowstring or any other sling or strap from slipping off your shoulder, sparing you the trouble of constantly repositioning the sling or strap.

I have antler buttons on all my outerwear, from parka to chamois shirt. A simple button would also work, but the antler looks better and draws more comments.

Henry Trefethen
Somersworth, New Hampshire

FRESH PINE SCENT

To keep my clothes smelling like the woods, I go to a Christmas tree lot and pick up discarded tree trimmings. After washing my hunting clothes in a scent-free detergent, I place them in a large rubber storage tote that is layered with these branches. The result is pine-scented hunting clothes!

Mel Jellison Jr.
Iselin, New Jersey

PLASTIC TUBS CONTROL SCENT

For controlling scent, start by buying two or three large plastic tubs that have strong, tight-clamping handles that lock the lids down tightly. (I recommend Rubbermaid's Action Packers.) When you purchase your tubs, grab several feet of $\frac{1}{4}$-inch-thick foam-rubber window seal stripping with an adhesive backing.

Once you get home, wash your tubs and lids with a scent-eliminating detergent and towel them dry. This removes most of the odor from the manufacturing process.

Once the tubs are dry, place the foam-rubber stripping along the tub's highest lip (do not place on the lid). Once this is complete, you have an airtight container in which you can stack and store clothing in your home or vehicle.

Vincent Butts
Tecumseh, Michigan

EASY DEER HAULER

To make a reliable deer cart, cut the front brace off an inexpensive plastic wheelbarrow, along with a portion of the forks in front of the wheel. Reattach the brace on top of the forks, and you have an excellent deer carrier. The absence of the front portion of the forks allows it to go over fallen logs and small rocks without catching.

Mike Weiss
Reese, Michigan

KEEP YOUR FEET WARM

My biggest concern while hunting in cold climates is keeping my feet warm. Once they're cold, I'm uncomfortable, and the cold creeps right up through me. I have tried various kinds of felt and other liners for my boots. They're usually too bulky, or they get wet and stay wet.

The best thing I have found is Sill Seal. It is a foam material about $\frac{1}{8}$ inch thick and is used in house building. (It is used between the foundation and sill to eliminate cold drafts.) I cut out pieces to cover the bottom of my boots, then place the pieces inside. Not only do they take up little room, but if they get wet, I just wipe them off with a dry rag.

Brent Foss
Southwest Harbor, Maine

GET THE ANGLE ON WARM FEET

This tip is directed at those who hunt from ground blinds or otherwise sit-and-wait while hunting in cold weather, and have had their patience and discipline tested by having their feet fall asleep, or have gotten cold despite expensive socks.

Here's the key thought. When standing, your feet are at a right angle (90 degrees) to your legs. Blood vessels run to and through the joints freely in this position. But when you sit inside a ground blind, with your knees and feet on the ground, or with your back against a tree while turkey hunting, your feet are hyperextended beyond their natural 90-degree angle, and if you are on an incline, this can easily exceed 135 degrees. When you do this, you're stretching the tissues in and around the joints of your ankles, and flattening them against the bones. This puts a lot of pressure on the blood vessels and nerves, which cuts off circulation, causing your feet to get cold, and sometimes even pinches nerves, causing your feet to fall asleep.

When your ankle is flexed beyond 90 degrees, blood flow to your feet and toes is restricted. Result: cold feet, miserable hunt.

Here's an easy fix: Find a couple of rocks, small logs or branches (or whatever you can find) that are about 2 to 4 inches thick—depending on the size of your feet—and place them under the toes of your boots to elevate the front of your feet so your ankle is bent in its natural, relaxed, 90-degree position. This will keep your feet warm and awake!

This tip is based on a combination of 13 years of medical experience, as well as field trial and error.

Frank Vozenilek
Cedar Rapids, Iowa

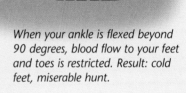

Rest your foot on a rock or branch, bringing your ankle back to a 90-degree angle so that blood flows freely. Result: warm feet, enjoyable hunt.

TURKEY

If turkeys were cigarettes, we'd all smoke.

That's how addictive these big birds are. Talking to them with your calls, convincing a *wild* turkey to come on in … once you've hunted spring gobblers or experienced the fun of chasing fall birds, you're a goner.

Here's what your brethren have to say about the turkey hunting addiction. And it's some good stuff.

How'd I Miss ?!

I will never forget one spring turkey season when I missed the easiest shot I've ever had. I had been working a group of toms for about an hour. After some intense conversation, the birds went silent, telling me they were on their way. After another 20 minutes of nerve-racking stillness, three toms appeared from over a terrace 20 yards away, so I had little time to position myself for a shot.

After all three toms looked at my decoy, they scrambled toward it in a frenzy of love. They passed less than 15 yards in front of me as I anxiously lined one up with the bead of my 12 gauge. After pulling the trigger and hearing the roar of my shot, I looked up expecting to see a turkey waiting to be tagged. Instead, all three toms flew into the deep blue of the morning sky, leaving me astonished at what had just occurred.

"There is no way I could have missed that shot,"

I thought to myself. I aimed my gun into the field, replaying the scenario. Was it nerves? Did I fail to aim true? Was there something wrong with my shotgun? Why I missed that turkey, I couldn't tell you for sure. It could have been a combination of things, or just one foolish error. However, if I had taken the time to properly prepare for that weekend, the story might have had a better ending.

We all make mistakes. But we become better by learning from any mistake. We all miss some shots, but there are ways to improve our odds of making a clean, humane kill. Here are six ways to ensure your next turkey shot is a good one.

Preparing

It's easy to get excited hours, days or even weeks before opening day. But take the time to check over your equipment before the season opens. Be sure to

No matter how good your calling skills, you will go home without a turkey if you miss your shot. The author has a plan for increasing your chances.

clean your gun, ensuring everything is in working order. This is where I could have discovered my first mistake in missing the turkey mentioned above. I had forgotten to change the choke in my 12 gauge shotgun. The last time I had used my shotgun was on a quail hunt. Forgetting that the improved-cylinder choke tube was still in the barrel, I shot a loose pattern of pellets at the wary tom. Always double-check your choke selection to ensure you're using at least a full-choke tube.

If you recently bought a firearm, take time to become familiar with it. Get a sense of how it feels, operates and shoots. This might seem obvious, but you would be surprised by how many hunters don't take the time to prepare, and it often costs them.

PATTERNING

Patterning is essential in preparing for turkey season. If I had patterned my shotgun before the above hunt, I would have likely realized my error before it was too late. Patterning a shotgun doesn't take much time, but many hunters overlook this crucial function. Each shotgun's pattern differs from the next, even if the guns are the same make and model.

To properly pattern your shotgun, try a variety of shell brands and shot sizes. Each type and brand will pattern differently. You want to find out which load puts the most pellets in the turkey's kill zone (neck and head area).

Shells commonly used for turkey hunting range from 2¾- to 3½-inch loads. Check your gun to see which length loads it can chamber. When selecting a load, use a brand you know. For turkey hunting, you'll want to stick with pellet sizes 4, 5 and 6.

Some hunters like No. 4 shot for its knockdown power, but others like No. 6 shot because it provides more pellets for a denser pattern. It's also possible to choose the No. 5 shot if you want a combination of power and pellet numbers. Don't limit yourself to regular loads for turkey hunting. Buy magnum shells designed for turkeys.

Many turkey guns now come with 3½-inch chambers, which can shoot shells with a high shot or pellet capacity. If your shotgun can fire 3½-inch loads, also fire some 3-inch shells. The smaller shells will sometimes shoot tighter patterns than

the larger shells, depending on the shotgun.

Set up a target at 20 yards. A target silhouette of a turkey's head is recommended to better show how many pellets strike the kill zone. It's a good idea to fire each load more than once to double-check its patterning abilities. Determine your maximum range as well.

POSITIONING

Another reason for missed shots is the hunter's position. Each hunter has a different shooting style. Some are happy setting up in a blind where they believe turkeys are congregating. Others often set up against a wide tree or thick cover, while some move toward a vocal tom until they can set up for a shot. No matter what hunting style you prefer, it's important how you position for the bird.

Come spring, toms like open areas in woods or fields so they can see the hens they are seeking.

Plus, they can be on the lookout for danger.

If you set up in thicker cover, you increase the risk that a tom will hang up, and you limit your shooting lanes, which might force you to take a bad shot. If you plan to set up in the woods, find an area with open timber.

When possible, face downhill to give yourself a good view of the landscape.

It's vital to stay away from sites that limit your view, such as dense woods, dips in the landscape, or terraces in fields. The sooner you can see the turkey, the less likely it will see you first. By spotting the turkey while it's a way off, you get more time to position yourself for a shot.

Getting comfortable and lining up the shot is crucial. Turkeys often seem to find a way to sneak up in the direction you least prefer. This often leads to hunters taking off-balance shots, which leads to bad sighting or improper shooting form, which causes misses.

SCENT CONTROL FOR TURKEY HUNTING?

We all know the importance of good camouflage and human scent elimination when hunting white-tailed deer. This same routine should be followed when turkey hunting.

Why should we worry about scent control when a turkey couldn't sniff us out if his life depended on it? Simply because deer and turkeys share the same habitat in most areas. Turkey hunters deal with enough obstacles without having their hunts cut short or disrupted by deer wandering by downwind, and then crashing and snorting off.

Turkeys tend to leave the area just as quickly after such sudden outbursts. And even if the turkeys are not frightened away, the disruption still forces a hunter to set up and try again. To me, it's much easier to try to avoid this situation!

Edward F. Wojcinski Jr.
Dundee, New York

Finally, because turkeys are unpredictable, make sure you can swivel your firearm freely. Do not set up where you can't turn one way or the other because trees, saplings or brush obstruct your movement.

LINING UP THE SIGHTS

Some products might help you line up your sights a little straighter and clearer. For traditionalists, a simple 12 gauge shotgun with a silver bead atop the muzzle is all they need.

But sometimes in the excitement before pulling the trigger on a longbeard, hunters concentrate more on the bird than lining up the bead flush with the barrel, thus causing them to shoot a foot high. Various shotgun sights can help you line up the gun more consistently.

One style of popular sights is the fiber-optic system, which absorbs available light to create a highly visible sight. These systems include rear and front sights, which help prevent shooters from firing left, right or above their target. Fiber-optic sights sometimes contain one flaw, however. When they are installed, they are not always lined up correctly. Be sure to fire a few rounds at a target to ensure accuracy.

Hunters who have trouble gauging distances might be uncomfortable lining up open sights. They might want to check out a scope designed for turkey hunting. Scopes allow a clear view of the target, and give a positive feel when lining up shots. Some scopes also help gauge distance with a specially designed crosshair that lets you know when the turkey is in range.

Although scopes allow more accurate shots, they have downsides. First, they cost more. Even though the cost is reasonable, fiber-optic sights or factory sights are far less expensive. Second, scopes must be sighted in each season. And finally, scopes limit your view. It's difficult to focus on your target in wooded areas, plus you cannot see what is going on around you.

If fiber-optics and scopes don't appeal to you, you can stick with iron sights. These sights resemble rifle sights, but are designed for shotguns. A rear and front iron sight help line up your target for more consistent shots.

Two beads work well too: One at the end of your

barrel, one midway down the rib. Simply line them up to be sure you're not shooting high or low.

JUDGING DISTANCE

Shooting distances play a big role in tagging wild turkeys. With more powerful ammunition and improved sighting systems, many hunters will try longer shots. I have taken a couple of longbeards at about 40 yards, but for two reasons only. One, I was confident in my shotgun's pattern at that range. Two, the longbeards refused to approach any closer and began moving away.

I prefer to call in turkeys as close as possible, and hold off my shot until they are within 25 yards. (You don't want them too close, however; you'll have no pattern whatsoever and could more easily miss.) Not only is it exciting to watch turkeys at close range, but your odds for a clean shot rise with each step a turkey takes toward you. It's all about being patient and confident in your ability to stay still and concealed. Plus, a closer shot better ensures a quick, clean kill.

Like anything else, judging distances requires practice. Set up targets from the stand or sites you often hunt, or just use a field where you can safely practice shooting. Set three or four targets about 10 yards apart, up to 40 yards away. This helps you get an idea of how far a turkey is when it approaches. Then fire a round at each target to see how your shotgun patterns at different ranges.

BEATING TURKEY FEVER

After you've done all the preparations, the only challenge remaining is staying in control when that tom struts toward you. If you're like most hunters, your heart pounds rapidly, your palms sweat, and your nerves are shredded. In short, you have turkey fever.

What's the cure? Realistically, turkey fever is the adrenaline rush that brings us back to the woods and fields every spring. It's part of why we hunt!

The more you hunt, the more you learn to deal with this adrenaline jolt, but if hunting is in your blood, turkey fever will always be there in some form. When it occasionally ruins your ability to make the shot, don't get down. If you look forward to the rush instead of worrying about it, you'll likely be more successful in the years ahead.

Steve Bemke
Bridgeton, Missouri

CREATE A TURKEY HUNT MEMENTO

Here is an economical method to create a memento of a turkey, using its spurs, beard and the shell you used to take the bird.

After the harvest and the photos, remove the turkey's beard and spurs. Remove the beard by cutting around its base. To remove the spurs, cut the leg 1 inch above and below the spur. Put the spurs in a plastic sandwich bag with three tablespoons of salt for about a week to let them dry out.

After the spurs are dry, drill a ⅛-inch hole down through the leg to hollow it out. Place the hollowed-out spurs back into the bag of salt.

Get a spent shotshell (preferably the one you used on the turkey!) and turn it crimp side up. Fill the shell with two-part epoxy to ⅜ inch from the top of the crimp. Place the beard's root in the epoxy and let the shell cure for two days. After the epoxy cures in the shell, drill a ⅛-inch hole through the shell's brass.

Take a leather strip (from a craft store) or a leather shoelace and thread it through the shotshell, with the spurs on each side. Tie the lace off and you will have a keepsake of the hunt.

George Vamos
Mountain Top, Pennsylvania

BIRTH OF A TURKEY HUNTER

A few years ago, I spent a lot of time scouting for the spring gobbler season. I started scouting in mid-February and after 2½ months, I had a handful of birds behaving predictably once they flew down from the roost.

A friend was interested in joining me on opening day. He had hunted turkeys in the spring by himself, but had never had a serious encounter with a gobbler. I invited him to join me after telling him many of my successes and failures with these amazing birds. I could tell he didn't fully understand my enthusiasm and passion for this type of hunting.

Opening day found us where I wanted to be, 30 minutes before daybreak. We were hunting public land, and I knew we wouldn't be by ourselves for long. In the distance we could hear our camo-clad competition owl hooting and yelping already. My comrade, Greg, asked what I was waiting for.

"Too early," I said. "There's no pink in the horizon yet."

After another 15 minutes or so of this plastic-tubed owl hooting without hearing a gobble, I pointed to the eastern horizon and whispered, "It's time." I told Greg to face one direction and I'd face the other. I only wanted the tom to gobble one time, and we'd move in on him.

The beautiful jake kept coming in … and another turkey hunter was being born.

I cupped my hand to my mouth and let out an owl hoot. The gobbler responded immediately. He was roosted less than 150 yards downhill from us. I smiled and said, "Let's go get him!" As I turned and started walking away from the gobbler, Greg asked where we were going. I responded, "Where he's going."

Within a couple of minutes, we were set up on a small flat of hardwoods with patches of mountain laurel all around us. We were less than 10 yards apart, close enough to communicate with each other if we needed. I had just finished my fly-down cackle and had cleared the leaves from my feet when I noticed a long-legged jake on a dead run heading toward us from about 100 yards away.

I had to move around the tree to get the right shooting angle, and I had to get Greg to move also. I motioned for him to move like I had and to get ready. From the look in his eyes, I knew he hadn't seen this jake yet. He repositioned and took my lead. When he saw me staring down my barrel, he decided to do the same.

I always wanted to be the first one to shoot on an opening morning of spring gobbler season. But having Greg pull the actual trigger would be fine with me!

The jake was on the move, now within 70 yards of us, looking for the hen he had just heard fly down. His 4-inch beard was easy to see as he cautiously continued toward us. He would walk a few steps, stop and stretch his head straight up, looking. Some large rocks were between us and the bird. I wondered if Greg saw him yet. If so, I hoped he would wait and not try to shoot too far. The night before and earlier that morning I kept telling him, "30 yards or less, 30 yards."

Finally the jake got within 30 yards of me and he was still coming. Then it was 25 and then 20. He finally stopped about 15 yards in front of us and I waited for Greg's 10 gauge to break the morning's silence.

"WWWHOOOOOMM!"

I was on top of that bird before the shotgun's roar stopped echoing off the mountain! I looked back at Greg, and I could tell by his football-sized eyes that another turkey hunter had been born.

About an hour later, Greg's hands were still shaking after the long walk back to the cabin. It's amazing how a turkey can turn a 35-year-old man to mush. Thank you, Greg, for one of my greatest moments in the incredible, adrenaline-filled sport of turkey hunting!

Robert C. Meyers
Wind Gap, Pennsylvania

DECOY/STRING SETUP

When setting up a turkey decoy, there is an easy way to control the decoy's movement.

Most hunters stand two sticks on both sides of the rear of the decoy so the wind won't keep spinning the decoy around.

A better way is to take several yards of light fishing line and thread it through the decoy's beak. Use a needle to pull the thread through, and then tie a knot at the end. Use a tent stake about 8 to 10 inches long, and place it about 3 feet in front of the decoy to hold the line close to the ground. Extend the fishing line to your hiding place. Just a slight tug on the line every few minutes makes the decoy appear to be feeding, or at least moving. And doing so from the front of the decoy keeps it facing you, like you want.

Any incoming turkey will circle the decoy to get face to face with it, and this will bring the turkey in close enough for a shot. Also, its back will be momentarily to you, allowing you to move your gun (if necessary) without being detected.

This setup worked for me the first time I tried it. After only a few yelps and clucks, my bird came within 10 yards for an easy shot. And, with this setup you control the decoy's movement, instead of being at the wind's mercy.

Gabriel L. Escobar
Tucson, Arizona

A simple setup using fishing line and a tent stake can help you give realistic feeding-action life to a decoy ... and bring the gobblers cruising in. Face the decoy toward you and your hiding spot.

REELING IN TURKEYS

Take an ultralight fishing reel with you while turkey hunting, and attach its line to your decoy to provide movement. The reel eliminates tangles that you get from string or cord, and it is lightweight and easy to carry. Be sure to respool with new line before fishing because of nicks caused by sticks, stones and woodland debris.

Dean Wessels
Fairbury, Illinois

BE DIFFERENT
WHEN HUNTING SPRING GOBBLERS

When pursuing a mature gobbler, remember that he's probably heard and seen it all. After you try the traditional setups and they all fail, and your sweetest yelps shut him up, pull out a map and walk his turf to get to know it better.

If there's a road nearby, hunt him from the opposite direction. If he refuses to come up the hill to you, try calling him downhill.

Regardless of what the books and the old-timers say, gobblers will come downhill to you, even if they're with hens.

Do something he has not heard before. This will get his attention more than something he's heard over and over.

Try a box call. Not many turkey hunters still use box calls. Leave the yelps in the truck. He's heard those more times than you and I have. Use single clucks or a few short rapid clucks and wait. Remember that last time you sneaked within 150 yards of a loudmouth gobbler near a powerline or dirt road? As soon as you gave him your sexiest yelp, he shut his mouth for the day. That's because turkeys cannot gobble when they're laughing!

Robert C. Meyers
Wind Gap, Pennsylvania

STRING KEEPS TABS ON STRIKERS

To prevent losing my striker when hunting turkeys, I drill a small hole in the striker handle. I then attach a string to it, and tie it to my slate call. When I'm ready to leave, I always have my striker with me.

Christie Berg
Logan, Kansas

DON'T STRIKE OUT

When using slate-type friction calls, make sure you have several different types of strikers with different tones. If you find a gobbler is hanging up, switch to another striker to sound like another hen. This could excite the tom and bring him closer.

John D. Fallon
Doylestown, Pennsylvania

Sleep-deprived turkey hunters, both spring and fall, are known to lose gear all over the woods. To keep track of your striker, attach it to your slate or glass call with a string.

BROTHERLY LOVE IN THE TURKEY WOODS

When it comes to deer hunting, I admit my brother is a more skillful hunter than I am. But when it comes to turkeys, it's a different story. I seem more skillful. Or lucky, as he describes it.

I have been successful the three times I have drawn a turkey tag. He has yet to bag a turkey after about eight attempts. I frequently remind him of these statistics, and he offers no defense.

On a recent opening morning, I set up in the dark but I didn't like my spot once the sun came up. Shortly after, I heard two gobbles: one in front and one behind. I left my spot and went after the bird behind me. I set up in the corner of a freshly planted soybean field that borders a large forest of oaks. I set out my decoy in the field, and hid in the brush along the fenceline.

A hen soon came out of the woods and entered the field about 150 yards from me. A bit later, a strutting tom came out and joined her. As I watched the tom, I heard a different gobbler. As the hen and strutting tom worked their way to an island of trees in the middle of the field, another bird ran from the woods to the island.

I scratched my call, but all three birds seemed to ignore me and my decoy. I was thinking about how I would set up the next day, when the gobbling tom left the island and headed toward the fenceline behind me. He made it to the fence and started gobbling again. The hen and strutting tom eventually followed.

Thinking I had missed my chance, I leaned out and peeked down the fenceline. The hen was still in the field. I leaned back and continued calling, hoping to get her attention and have some fun. Then I caught movement in the corner of my eye. She was about 5 feet behind me. I must have flinched, because she got nervous and moved away from the fenceline. However, she continued moving toward my decoy while making soft, cautious putts. I decided to talk back to her, imitating her the best I could.

Suddenly my conversation with the hen was shattered by a gobble about 20 yards away. After gathering my composure, I slowly turned. The tom was coming up the field road toward the hen and decoy.

I was not concealed well from that direction, so I waited for the tom to walk behind the brush in front of me before raising my gun. As he got there, I looked and saw the strutting tom approaching. Although the gobbling tom could not see me, I was in full view of the strutter.

Should I risk raising my gun in plain view of the strutter? I decided he was concentrating so hard on the other tom, hen and decoy that I could get away with it. I slowly raised my gun, drew a bead on the gobbler's head as he walked out into the field, and pulled the trigger. The gobbler dropped.

To my surprise, the strutter ran to my bird and beat on him with all he had! As feathers were flying, I jumped out of the brush and approached. The strutter did not even notice me. He continued beating my bird with his wings and legs. Mike Tyson would have been impressed! Finally, the strutter jumped off and flew away.

I gathered my gear and proudly carried my heavy tom back to the house. When I arrived, I had to call my brother, who was at work. I told him, "Hey, I need to get a four-wheeler so I can haul these heavy turkeys out of the woods!"

Now, I doubt those two toms were brothers, but it makes me wonder what would happen if I pass on before my brother. After witnessing what happened to my bird, maybe I should let up on him. Nah, it's too much fun!

Ben Street
Bloomington, Minnesota

Turkeys Are Smart, Turkeys Are Dumb

Are turkeys smart or are they dumb? It depends on who you talk to. I believe turkeys are not that smart. They spend their entire lives with someone or something trying to kill them. To reach adulthood, they must instead be wary and quick.

I've hunted turkeys for most of 40 years. I sometimes think I have made all the mistakes you can make while turkey hunting, but then I make a new one. I wish I knew how many turkeys I have called up and let get away. For that matter, I wish I knew how many I have killed. Many of those that got away simply had more patience than I had, and I spooked them when I got up to leave.

Calling is 90 percent of turkey hunting. Or is woodsmanship and setting up 90 percent of turkey hunting? There again, it depends on who you talk to.

I couldn't get to first base in a turkey-calling contest, but I'm not out to impress a bunch of men. I just want to impress gobblers, and I'm a fair hand at that.

One good example of why I don't think turkeys are so smart is this: My turkey hunting buddy Glen and I once went to a field where we had seen turkeys many times and had killed a few. I set up in some bushes at the edge of the woods and Glen set up across a narrow part of the field about 200 yards away. At first light, I made my calls and tried to judge some distances to where I could kill a turkey if one came in.

About 35 yards away, there was a terrace that ran

When hunting turkeys, you're up against incredible wariness more than anything else.

parallel with the woods. The turkey flew out into the field, gobbled and came walking down that terrace. When he reached the point of my mental marker, I fired the 3-inch magnum with copper-plated No. 4s. I didn't cut a feather, and the gobbler ran back the way he had come, clucking loudly all the way, and went out of sight behind some bushes to my left. It was still early, so I waited a few minutes and made another call. Unknown to me, but in full view of Glen, that turkey turned around and came back down the terrace to the spot where I had missed him. The problem was, I didn't expect him back and he saw me first as I sprayed for mosquitoes. He again ran away, clucking as he went.

My dad was a turkey hunter when I was a boy, but had quit by the time I was ready to get serious about hunting. He said many times that if a turkey answers your call from fairly close, he will come in sometime that day to check out that hen. Dad said the tom might go the other way or he might leave with hens, but sooner or later he would come back, "so just put your yelper away and get your gun ready and be patient."

One day a couple of seasons ago I called to a fairly vocal gobbler. He would come within about 50 yards and then go back the other way. I couldn't see him because of the brush, so I figured he couldn't see me, either. I decided to move up to where he last came.

When he gobbled going away, at what seemed

to be about 200 yards, I moved up. When I got to the place I wanted and set up, I made a loud call that some of the experts term an assembly yelp. I call it a "lost call." Then I said to myself, "He'll be back and I'll be here waiting." I slid down on the ground with my head on my pack and immediately went to sleep.

I don't know what woke me 45 minutes later. Maybe it was a sound, but it was not a gobble. I opened my eyes while lying still, and there stood the gobbler 15 yards in front of me. As he walked behind a tree about 30 yards away, I raised up on an elbow and let him have the load of No. 4s. He was a great turkey with a 10½-inch beard and 1-inch spurs.

No trick and no call will work every time with turkeys, but some things will work every time if conditions are right. One trick I use is this: When I think I am in the woods close to a roosting gobbler, I wait until first light. I prefer the period when it's too early for a turkey to be on the ground, but hopefully after he has completed his wake-up gobbling on the roost. Then I make a soft tree yelp, wait a couple of minutes, and then do a fly-down cackle. I then wait a couple of minutes and do my "lost call." If his hens don't fly down first, or he gets spooked or suspicious about some noise or movement, he'll hit the ground coming to your call. I've killed turkeys after being in the woods no more than 30 minutes using this method.

Another trick I use later in the day is best for when I spot or hear turkeys. I set up first, and then use a slate or glass to make a loud cutt. I follow that with a loud lost call on my mouth diaphragm. I've watched more than once as a turkey did a 180-degree turn and came to me after I made these calls.

I love turkey hunting. I will not shoot one over bait or off the roost. I enjoy the hunt, whether I kill a turkey or not. I once read somewhere this quote: "I don't hunt to kill, I kill to have hunted." That fits me to a T.

Gary Faust
Red Level, Alabama

SCOUT TURKEYS SMARTLY

When turkey hunting, scout the area you'll be hunting to find the natural routes the turkeys use. They have preferred travel routes. If you locate a bird, you can set up a blind on a route you have found. This increases your odds for a close encounter.

Robert J. Manske
Portage, Wisconsin

USE 2 OR 3 TURKEY CALLS

During the spring turkey hunting season, use two or three different calls at the same time. For example, a mouth call, box call and a glass slate make a good trio. This often brings the toms running.

Chris Hausher
Oologah, Oklahoma

CALLING TACTICS FOR GOBBLERS

A stubborn gobbler will sometimes find it worth his while to check out two hens instead of one, so try imitating two different birds by using a friction call along with a mouth call. If he still hangs up, use a weak gobble followed by a few slow jake yelps to fire him up. He will think a satellite jake has moved in to steal the girls.

Robert Davis
Mount Pleasant, Pennsylvania

LATE CAN BE DOUBLY GOOD

Nothing is more exhilarating than opening day of spring turkey season, except maybe anticipating it. With winter vanishing around the corner, one thing remains constant in my one-track mind: the beautiful sound of a lovesick tom on a lovely spring morning.

Last April, I was quietly fishing for largemouth on a farm pond when the gobble of a far-off tom broke the silence soon after sunrise. Before long, one tom after another broke into song, their orchestrated love cries echoing back and forth throughout the Missouri hillsides.

My diaphragm call was still in my jacket pocket from the day before, when I was brushing up on my calling. I couldn't resist, so I slipped the call from its case and into my mouth. I whispered a few sleepy yelps, followed by a few affectionate purrs. Bam! I nearly jumped out of my boat as a nearby tom answered from the nearby woods.

For amusement, I carried on a short conversation, but this tom hung around his roost, asking me to join him and the rest of his sweethearts. I pleasantly declined and went on with my fishing, anticipating opening day more than ever.

Each day preceding opening day seemed an eternity, but the magical day finally arrived and my eyes slowly adjusted to the hazy numbers on the alarm clock. Something was very wrong. Sunshine was pouring through my window! After a brief, derogatory exchange with the alarm clock, I assembled my gear and headed out to my faithful spot at 8:15 a.m.

As I headed into a field about 200 yards from my blind, I let out some yelps followed by several cutts, hoping to locate a nearby tom. As I stopped to listen, only distant crows broke the silence.

I eventually reached my blind and set up a couple of hen decoys and offered some more yelps and cutts. A couple of hours passed, and I still had not heard a tom's faintest response. Yesterday morning I had sat outside and listened to toms call all over the area. Some days they just don't gobble.

It was now nearly 11 a.m., and it didn't seem any turkeys were going to come my way, so I headed in for breakfast. I packed away my decoys, and as I started back to the house, I gave one last call. I couldn't believe my ears. Sure enough, a faint gobble floated my way.

Late can be great. Late in the morning when the sun is up, and late in the season when everything is green and leafed out, can both be excellent times to tag a tom.

"Okay, better late than never," I thought. Again I called with some yelps. But as soon as I belted out some cuts, he gobbled one after another. Each time I called back he responded immediately, and each time he answered he was getting louder.

I was stunned at the gobbler's approach speed. After hours of silence, this tom was coming at me like he had never seen a hen in his life. I quickly moved to a patch of timber where I could set up. I was watching a long hill that stretched 300 yards to the next property. When I offered some soft purrs, he gobbled back, still rapidly closing the distance.

I didn't have long to set up, but as I glanced to my left, I realized I was in trouble if he came from that direction. A wall of thick brush and a small ravine would bring this hunt to a disappointing conclusion if I didn't act fast. I called again with my diaphragm call, this time cupping my mouth and turning my head to the right to try and lead the eager tom where I wanted him.

Just as I was about to let out my final yelps, not one but two crimson heads jutted above the crest of a terrace 50 yards away. Like two ghosts appearing out of nowhere, these two toms defined the nickname "longbeards." My heart was already pounding, but now the words "heart attack" were crossing my mind.

I would love to tell you one of the two trophy toms now sits atop my fireplace, but that's not what happened. Instead, they walked to my left and disappeared behind the ravine. I was left with nothing but a weak heart after a quick but exciting encounter with the birds.

The lesson? It's important not to be discouraged early in the morning if you do not get any responses. More than likely, the toms hear your calls but are preoccupied by hens they roosted with the evening before. Until they are finished breeding those hens, your calls might not be acknowledged until later in the morning.

Fortunately, I was able to provide a Mother's Day turkey later that season. The late season is a great time to tag a tom, because many hens have been bred and are sitting on their nests. This leaves toms with fewer hens to chase around.

It's important not to get discouraged from turkey hunting just because you have a little bad luck early in the day, or early in the season. Sit tight, hunt hard and your chances will come.

And be sure to double-check your alarm clock the evening before!

Steve Bemke
Bridgeton, Missouri

CAMO FOR TURKEY HUNTING

I like to break up my colors and camo patterns for spring turkey hunting. I find it most effective to use a fall pattern like Realtree Xtra Gray for my pants, and Mossy Oak Green Leaf or Shadow Leaf patterns on my upper body. This not only breaks up my silhouette, but the pants' autumn colors match the dead leaves and limbs, while the upper spring colors match the underbrush and emerging leaves.

Michael Denham
Marseilles, Illinois

The author displays a good gobbler that found out the hard way how effectively a "two-tone" camo plan can hide a spring hunter.

PERSISTENCE PAYS OFF FOR TURKEYS

During my first few years trying to bag a gobbler, I learned a couple of important things about turkeys and hunting them.

First, you must find out where they are. That means scouting a short time before your season opens. I've scouted a spot several weeks in advance, only to return later and find the turkeys had moved on or had become call-shy because other hunters had been there ahead of me.

That doesn't mean you won't see turkeys there. One year I found a small piece of state land with several toms in the area. When I returned to hunt, I found lots of tire tracks and footprints, and could not locate a bird anywhere. I didn't go back for a couple of days, and was almost surprised when I blew on my crow call just before daylight. At least two toms were roosting within 100 yards of me!

I set up at the base of a hill on an old two-track that ran along the edge of a swamp. After the gobblers left the roost, I never heard them again. Still, I sat for a while and called occasionally.

Finally, I decided it was time to move on and started to get up. A tom took off just above me on the hill and flew out of sight into the swamp.

I don't know where he came from, but I never heard him and he definitely wasn't one of the birds I originally heard. Had I been more patient, I might have had a shot at that bird. A couple of days later, I returned to the same area and was calling to a distant tom that answered my every call. He was on private property, so I set up my decoys and sat down to see if he might come to me.

We probably called to each other for about 30 minutes, and he wasn't getting any closer. Just when I figured it was a lost cause, I heard a noise behind me. It turned out to be a big tom that was

Be persistent, and don't become discouraged if toms don't gobble madly back at your calls. Pressured birds will often come in very cautiously, and very silently. Be ready.

strutting in the two-track about 50 yards behind me. (I later found his tracks and drag marks from his wings in the sand.) I never would have known that bird was there if he hadn't walked off the road and crunched the dry leaves as he came up behind me. I couldn't get my gun turned around without being seen, and he eventually walked out of range.

I didn't get a shot at that bird, but it really made me wonder how many toms will check out hen calls without making a sound.

If you know birds are around and they have been hunted and spooked, it probably pays to spend extra time to let a silent old tom come and check you out.

On another morning, I was walking and calling, trying to locate a bird when I heard a hen clucking on the next ridge. I sat down and we called back and forth for several minutes. I hoped that maybe a gobbler was with the hen, but she just kept walking back and forth on the opposite ridge, talking back to me. I sat and tried to imitate her calls when I suddenly heard several gobbles from behind me. I foolishly tried to get turned around, but those two toms topped the hill behind me just as I was settling back down. I got a good look at the lead gobbler's beard as he ran down the side of the hill and out of sight.

I wanted to kick myself for moving when I did, but if I had not stayed and called to that lone hen, I doubt I would have ever known those two toms were around. It sure didn't hurt to have a live hen calling with me.

I hunted for several years before I finally shot my first gobbler. If you pay attention to what goes wrong when a bird spooks, you might be able to avoid those mistakes in the future. If you are persistent, sooner or later everything will come together, and that big tom will walk into range of your shotgun.

My first gobbler had an 8-inch beard and weighed almost 25 pounds. He never answered my calls until after I had five jakes gobbling around me for almost 15 minutes. Those jakes stayed around as long as I called. When they walked away, I would call them back. They never stopped gobbling as long as I was calling to them.

After several minutes, I heard another bird gobbling. He eventually joined with the jakes just out of range. As soon as I called again, one of the jakes gobbled and started to come back toward me. The big tom didn't like that, and chased the jake away. Then he walked toward me and I dropped him at 25 yards with a load of 6s.

James Kushner
Charlevoix, Michigan

DUCK CALLS ARE GOOD SHOCK CALLS

The next time you go preseason scouting, don't forget to take your favorite duck call. That's right, a duck call! Hail calls work the best to shock toms into gobbling. Believe me, you'll get some really strange looks from your seasoned turkey hunting friends. The only thing stranger will be the expressions on their faces when you get birds gobbling at your hail calls. This works in the morning, midday and all afternoon. Then compare vests once the next hunting season begins. Your friends will probably have a duck call stashed inside a pocket too.

Robert C. Meyers
Wind Gap, Pennsylvania

PATIENCE REQUIRED

If you have plenty of patience, and you are set up in a good spot where you are concealed, and you are hearing turkeys gobble, stay put. Sooner or later, that old tom will probably give in and start looking for that pesky hen that won't come to him.

Gene Heisler
Pawnee, Oklahoma

THE ABCs OF TURKEY HUNTING

Always make sure of your target.

Be familiar with your firearm.

Camouflage yourself completely.

Devote yourself to the hunt.

Expect the unexpected.

Force yourself to remain still.

Give that turkey time to get within range.

Hunt where the turkeys are.

Introduce a youngster to turkey hunting.

Join the National Wild Turkey Federation.

Keep a record of your hunt.

Listen for turkeys going to roost at dusk.

Master your calling technique.

Never aim for the body of a turkey.

Obey all game laws.

Preserve our turkey hunting heritage.

Quell the urge to call too loudly or too often.

Respect the landowner's rights.

Select a good calling site.

Turn in all poachers.

Use all of your woodsman's skills.

Value the outdoor experience.

Weather the weather.

Xmas can come early in the turkey woods.

Your homework is done, enjoy the hunt.

Zero hour is when that gobbler steps into view.

Michael Williams
Poultney, Vermont

REALISTIC EYES FOR TURKEY DECOYS

To make a turkey decoy more realistic—whether it's a jake, hen or strutting jake—get black fingernail polish and paint the eyes. It makes the eyes look realistic, and I think that's important because turkeys are like people in that they make eye contact.

Kenny Crummett
Sugar Grove, West Virginia

Decoy with painted (left) and unpainted eye. Which looks more real?

The tools of the trade are simple.

WHITETAIL TACTICS FOR FALL TURKEYS

One of the best ways to hunt fall turkeys is to use the same tactics we've used for years on white-tailed deer. One tactic that crosses over effectively is placing one or more companions along the escape route of a scattered flock.

Once we have patterned a flock, we can flush the birds from a feeding area and they will consistently fly to the same general area. After they land, the stander can call them to regroup. Sometimes they will actually surround the stander upon landing. The results of this technique vary.

Last fall, my brother and I located a flock that was visiting a beef farmer's grain feeding area at the edge of a feed lot at the same time each day. When flushed, the birds always flew about 500 yards south across pastures and hayfields to a swampy, wooded area.

I dropped my brother off near the swamp and, after waiting 10 minutes for him to walk in and take a position, I drove over to the feed lot and then walked toward the birds until they took flight. As planned, they flew across the fields and over the hill right to the swamp where my brother was waiting. I circled back around to where I had dropped off my brother, and quietly entered the lower end of the area. By this time, he was talking to the birds, and they were responding. He quickly selected a bird and made a clean shot.

I then waited about 10 minutes and began calling. I immediately heard birds moving through the brush toward me. After making a few more soft calls, I heard them softly calling back and moving closer. Three birds appeared all at once. I shifted slightly, and made a one-shot harvest in short order.

The farmer who had given us permission to hunt had heard the shots and was waiting when we walked out. He was astounded that we had gotten two birds so quickly. From start to finish, we had taken 45 minutes.

There are three keys to making this tactic work. First, find a flock and pattern its movements. Next, watch the birds to see where they flee from the flush site. Finally and most important, when flushing, spook the birds enough to make them take flight as a group, but not so fast that they scatter in all directions instead of going where they normally prefer. The best way to prevent a wild flush is to walk toward the birds like the farmer replenishing the feed tubs. I have even carried a bucket with a few stones in it to rattle as I walk.

We have all set up along escape routes and put on drives, or waited for other hunters to push deer past us. In a way, that's what we do with this method.

If you try this method, I think you will find it consistently successful.

Roy Dust
Camden, New York

POSITION DECOYS PROPERLY

When using decoys for spring gobblers, make sure they're in an open spot where a gobbler can see them. Also, face the decoy away from the direction you expect the tom to come from. If the decoy is not facing the gobbler, he will "chase" it, because he assumes the decoy is moving away. If the decoy is facing the gobbler, he might strut out of shooting range, expecting the hen to follow him.

Robert C. Meyers
Wind Gap, Pennsylvania

TWIST TIES AID FIELD DRESSING

When dressing your turkey, after cutting the rectum free, take a wire twist tie and secure it around the open end. This prevents fecal matter from slipping out and contaminating the meat.

Dean Wessels
Fairbury, Illinois

BIG GAME

There's a whole continent of wonderful big game out there.

That's what we celebrate here. Moose, pronghorns, black bears, mule deer and others ... some of us are fortunate to hunt these creatures almost in our backyard, some of us have to travel to enjoy hunting them.

Either way, the ideas here will make you a better big game hunter, and help you understand the allure of hunting these magnificent animals.

REAL HUNTING SUCCESS

Whether a big game hunt is enjoyable and becomes "food for the soul" depends on the hunter's attitudes and beliefs about hunting. What follow are a few thoughts that might help you reexamine and reevaluate your hunting experiences.

Avoid getting caught up in competition. This problem is most evident among hunters who seem driven to find a trophy. While it is certainly a thrill to take an animal with oversized horns or antlers, a consuming desire to take a particular type of animal can prevent a hunter from enjoying the hunt.

If you cannot ignore your competitive nature, view the hunt as competition between you and the animal, and not as competition between you and other hunters.

Honor and respect the animal you are hunting. If you kill an animal, realize it has given its life so you can eat. Honor the animal by not wasting any meat. Let the eating of the animal remind you that all life is interconnected and interdependent, and that you are also part of nature and the cycle of life and death.

If you can find satisfaction in just being outdoors, appreciating the beautiful places our sport takes us, then you've found real hunting success.

Native Americans have a tradition of praying over an animal they kill. They give thanks to the Creator for providing the animal, and they thank the animal for giving its life so they can eat and live. All hunters would do well to adopt this tradition as a way of honoring the animals they hunt.

While looking for an animal, be sure to also look at all the other plants and animals and experience the wonderful sights and sounds available to those who spend time in the outdoors. Do not allow yourself to become so preoccupied with finding an animal that you forget to notice and enjoy the sunrise and sunset, the changing seasons and changing weather, the hills, mountains, streams and all living things.

A trophy is a memento or symbol of a successful hunt. Given that definition, every animal, regardless of size, is a trophy—if it was taken in fair chase during an ethical and legal hunt. And if you broaden your definition of a successful hunt, a photograph and even a colorful stone or a bit of moss-colored bark collected during a hunt becomes a trophy if it reminds you of the success you had enjoying the outdoors at a particular time and place.

Charles R. Horejsi
Missoula, Montana

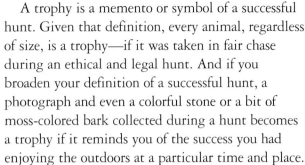 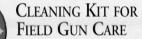

CLEANING KIT FOR FIELD GUN CARE

I carry an emergency gun cleaning kit in my shirt pocket. The container is a metal sore-throat lozenges box.

Inside is a 1- to 2-ounce plastic bottle filled with gun oil; a coiled length of stiff, rubber-coated automotive wire about 4 feet in length; several cotton swabs; several strips of Scotch tape inside the lid; and about 4 feet of nylon fishing line with a nail tied to one end and a small rag on the other.

If dirt or debris gets into my barrel, this kit may cure the problem in the field. Uncoil the stiff automotive wire and use as a light-duty ramrod to poke a path through the barrel. Then drop the fishing line down the barrel with the nail acting as the weight. The attached piece of rag acts as a cleaning swab. Use the oil to help clean, and it also will act as protection against rust and moisture. Use the spare strips of Scotch tape to retape the gun's muzzle to prevent further problems with barrel obstructions.

James R. Shewfelt
Sherwood Park, Alberta

STICK TO YOUR GAME PLAN FOR MOOSE

I have hunted many types of animals here in the North, but I primarily hunt for moose. By using strategies I have learned through trial and error, I harvest a moose almost every year.

Years ago, I would drive as far from civilization as possible to hunt, but after realizing a lot of my hunting time was wasted in getting to my destination, and finding more and more people also driving to those same places, I tried hunting within a one-hour radius of my home.

While berry-picking with my family one late-summer evening, I sat on a hill to look at the view. From where I sat, I could see many square miles of forest. Sitting a while longer, I started to see moose browsing in pockets of willows that were not visible from any other vantage point. That fall when hunting season opened, I was seated on that point at first light, and again moose were in the same pockets. Because I mainly hunt for meat, the choice was easy. After a short stalk and a well-placed shot, my moose was down.

This has happened smoothly for many years, and even my wife, two brothers and my father—who

usually help retrieve the moose—have taken many moose from this area. The same area has produced many prize bulls for us, while many of my friends drive miles and miles and see nothing.

Moose tend to stay in the same area most of their lives. We have seen the same bulls year after year. They are distinguished by certain antler traits or tears in their ears. Three years ago, my younger brother shot at a nice bull in a willow thicket, but it trotted off, leaving hardly a drop of blood. After examining the area where it was standing, we noticed a broken willow branch that must have deflected the bullet. Extensive tracking revealed no other sign of a hit. We saw the same moose a few more times that year, but could not get it. The following two years were the same. We would spot it with other moose, but could not harvest it.

"The next year" came, and I was fortunate to get a late draw license. My brothers and my father hunted the same area during the first season and all three got respectable moose. When the late season opened, the first snowfall found me on my perch. The snow must have been a good omen, because I

FIELD DRESSING ELK, MOOSE

When field dressing large animals like elk, moose and caribou, it is imperative that you cut the hide at the back of the neck, just as you would cape it for a head mount. Lay it open to get air to the meat so it will cool. If this is not done, even in cold weather, the meat could spoil. A friend lost 15 pounds of meat because he didn't follow this procedure.

Don Wallis
Citrus Heights, California

BUTCHER BIG PIECES

Here is a tip for do-it-yourself butchering. Cut the meat into roasts, cut the backstraps into long roasts, and save scraps for stew meat, hamburger or sausages. When you defrost your roasts, you can still cut butterfly steaks out of backstraps and so on. This will save butchering time and keep meat from freezer burning, because less of the meat's surface area is exposed when it freezes.

Brian A. Parks
Rock Springs, Wyoming

The author with a good late-season moose that his family knew well ... and that took several seasons to get.

saw him: the same moose we had been seeing for three years. He was 200 yards away, herding nine cow moose, along with two other young bulls. I took a shot and he was down instantly. While skinning him, I found an old 7mm bullet mushroomed just under the skin. It was proof that my brother had hit the willow branch and had not wounded the bull seriously.

I hunt mainly with a .30-06 with handloads and find they have plenty of knock-down power on large moose, as long as the shot is placed in the chest cavity. Good binoculars and spotting scopes are a must, because moose tend to blend into their environment and are hard to spot. You can look over an area five times and suddenly, there they are.

Rangefinders are also a great asset in open clearcuts. Because moose body sizes vary, distance can be hard to judge and hunters can be easily fooled.

Camouflage clothing is nice, but not necessary, because moose seem to pick up on movement even at great distances. I have had cow moose spot me at 1,000 yards and bolt. Stalking behind ridges or rows of trees is a must.

Calling moose works well because moose tend to be very sociable animals. The exception is late in the year when mature bulls want to be alone and will not answer any calls. On the other hand, I have had moose come from more than a mile away to investigate my calls, and getting them into close range also makes retrieval easier. An exception to this rule is if there is plenty of cover. Stalking is a more favorable option because I would rather not put them on alert. They tend to look over the area intently when hearing a call. If they do not trust it, they simply disappear. Therefore, stalking is more favorable to me. But if it cannot be done, calling works as a second option.

One final tip is this: If you like to hunt moose and you are successful, stick to the same game plan and the same area. Learn the area inside and out, because the reasons you found one moose there will be the same reasons that keep other animals coming back year after year.

Harry Hofsink
Smithers, British Columbia

The author hunts territory he knows intimately, and he thinks every moose is a good moose.

AGGRESSIVE MOOSE HUNTING

I once called in a huge bull moose, but couldn't get him to come within range. I tried bull grunts (I usually just cow-call), racking willows and everything in my repertoire, but he still wouldn't budge. I thought maybe I should try going to him. So off I went, cow-calling as I moved toward him. I ended up shooting him at 25 yards!

After many more successful hunts with my rifle, bow and video camera, I've concluded that you don't need to be quiet as you move toward a bull. Anyone who has heard a cow moose walk through the bush knows how noisy they are! So, if a bull hangs up, put the pressure on him.

Rick Reid
Prince George, British Columbia

CHECKING A DOWNED ANIMAL

Approach a downed animal from the rear, step on its tail and roll it slightly under your foot. If there is any life at all, you will get a quick reflex. You can touch a near-dead animal anywhere on its body and it might not move. But just roll your foot on its tail, and I guarantee if there is any response left in the animal, this will produce it. Everyone should use this technique before trying to put a knife into a big game animal.

Archie Kalkbrenner
Centerville, Pennsylvania

BEAT FATIGUE

Hunting elk and mule deer can be exhausting. It often requires miles of walking each day, usually in steep country. Unfortunately, many of us are not in the physical shape we would like. Even if we are in shape, fatigue and muscle aches are problems we need to anticipate and prevent to the extent that it is possible. Here are a few suggestions:

• Drink plenty of water all day long. Adequate water intake lessens muscle fatigue and is essential to efficient body functioning.

• Use a walking stick. The added support it provides can prevent much body twisting and reduce strain of the large muscles. An old ski pole makes an excellent and inexpensive walking stick. Collapsible walking sticks that fit into a daypack can be purchased at stores that handle backpack-

ing equipment. Some serious hikers use two poles in rough or slippery terrain.

• Wear a wide support belt—similar to the ones worn by weightlifters or people who do a lot of lifting on their jobs—to help prevent fatigued back muscles.

• Snack lightly all day. Candy bars are okay and convenient, but a much better choice is a mix of nuts, dried fruit like raisins, and small M&M candies. This mix is often called "gorp." Be sure to drink plenty of water with these snacks.

• During a day-long hunt, take time out from walking to sit. You might even nap for 30 minutes. A short nap can be surprisingly refreshing.

Charles R. Horejsi
Missoula, Montana

PERPENDICULAR CROSSHAIRS

You can improvise a gun vise by cutting notches into a sturdy box. To ensure the scope's crosshairs are true, level the rifle in the vise (box), and then sight through the scope to a level horizontal plane, such as a window ledge. Turn the scope to properly align the horizontal crosshair.

Toby Mohr
Manchester, Pennsylvania

When notched carefully, a sturdy cardboard box makes a passable gun vise for checking alignments and performing adjustments.

SECRETS FOR BUCKS & BULLS

I have always thought there are four key areas every hunter needs to be proficient in to ensure a successful hunt.

HUNT WHERE THE GAME IS

Many areas rarely or never contain game. Other areas nearby have game in them year after year. How do you find such areas? Scout! When you find an area with good sign, get to know it. I have three excellent areas to hunt deer and elk, and because I almost never hunt any other areas, I know these main areas inside and out. While hunting there, I

You can make your own hunting luck by doing your homework, and by just being in the woods … or mountains!

feel confident, because I know which places animals seek and which areas they avoid. This confidence stacks the deck in my favor to ensure a successful hunt.

MASTER YOUR SHOOTING

I believe in buying quality equipment, such as brand-name rifles, scopes, bases and ammunition.

Once you have the equipment, you must shoot often and from various positions to familiarize yourself with your firearm. If there is time, always find a rest for shooting at game. I recently started using a commercial set of shooting sticks that vastly improved my long-range shooting.

KNOW "THE RIGHT STUFF"

By "the right stuff," I mean woods savvy. A successful hunter knows to keep the wind in his face. He knows how to read sign. When he sees game, he knows whether to stalk closer or shoot from where he stands. He knows how to spot game, track game and precisely place the shot to ensure a quick kill. These are skills learned by practice, which means getting into the woods. Getting into the woods does not mean road hunting!

MAKE SOME LUCK

This is the final thing every hunter should have on his side, but unfortunately, it is the one thing he is least able to control: Make some luck. Without Lady Luck, even the best-laid plans can go awry. You can make your own luck, though, by doing your homework. Scout, familiarize yourself with your equipment, and gain experience by getting into the woods. It's always better to benefit from Lady Luck than suffer the consequences of Murphy's Law.

Phil Arnold
Garden Valley, Idaho

LINE UP THE RIBBON TO FIND DOWNED GAME

Here's a tip I use to locate downed game across a canyon. I take two sticks, tie surveyor's flagging on them, and line them up like a gun sight from where I shot to the animal. When I get to the other side of the canyon, the vegetation always looks different. I look back to where I shot from and walk until the two pieces of flagging are lined up. In many cases, I'm soon standing at the animal!

Ken Nelson
Astoria, Oregon

I once spotted a herd of elk on a mountainside about 200 to 250 yards away. I was finally able to shoot a cow. I knew where she fell from my position, so I tied a long, orange ribbon where my barrel was positioned, and another about 15 feet farther in line with the elk. I then climbed the mountain to the elk and, when I knew I was close, I used my binoculars to look at the ribbons. I was able to go left or right until I was lined up with the ribbons, and when I finally lined up, I looked down to see my elk. I don't know how much time I would have wasted without those two ribbons. Surveyor's tape works great too.

Brian A. Parks
Rock Springs, Wyoming

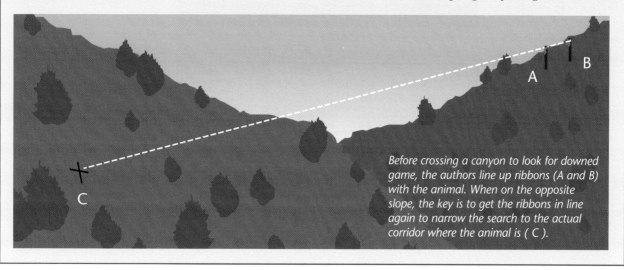

Before crossing a canyon to look for downed game, the authors line up ribbons (A and B) with the animal. When on the opposite slope, the key is to get the ribbons in line again to narrow the search to the actual corridor where the animal is (C).

ODOR CONTROL

Place a cup of baking soda in a cup or small bowl and place your hunting cap like a tent over it. Leave it there for two days. To increase odor control, lightly dust the cap with baking soda. And no, it will not harm your hair!

William Tong
Lufkin, Texas

Baking soda controls hat odor.

FLAG BEAR BAITING

I have several new ways to bait and hunt black bears. I call my first idea flag bear baiting.

When hunting in Quebec in the spring when the cover is thick, baiting is about the only way to get a look at a bear. When a bear is on a bait, you have time to judge its size as well as make a clean kill. I hunt around the edge of a lake that is about 5 miles long with several rivers and bays offering great bear baiting sites.

One successful hunt was with my nephew Gary. We had placed a bait on an old trail 200 yards up from the lake. The container of donuts had a small hole cut in its side so bears had to work to get the bait. We also dragged a grease bag a half mile on the trail to help lure a bear to the bait.

The bait was located in a slight dip. From the lake, we couldn't see the bait, so we tied

When he hits the bait, the flag goes down and the hunters move in.

a 6-foot-tall stick to the bait container and put a garbage bag on top for a flag. When we went fishing the next morning, we checked the bait. The flag was still in sight, so we went fishing. After fishing a couple of hours, we checked the flag

again—this time, the flag was gone. We made a stalk, and as we came into sight at about 50 yards, a really good bear sat up. Gary made a good shot, and we were soon crossing the lake with his trophy.

Another idea is to place the bait close enough to a lake so you can pull a line to a spot in sight of the lake. Pull a line over a limb, attach a weight to the flag, and put a band around the tree at the same height. Then fasten the line to a log propped over the bait container. When the bear knocks over the log, the flag will move up and down from the band around the tree. If you place the bait downhill, you can sneak to the top of the hill to make your shot.

You can go fishing within sight of the bait flag or check the bait flag every so often. You might even have several flags to watch. It is an exciting type of hunting, especially when the flag goes up and you move in. Sometimes, you might have to watch the bait if the bear is moving in and out, but it's still a great way to hunt black bears.

Tom Garvin
Rising Sun, Maryland

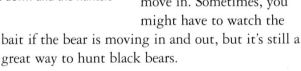

ALLURING SCENTS

Where legal for bear hunting, an effective scent can be made by putting bacon grease in a tin can and adding some anise food flavoring. Use a small can of Sterno fluid, put stones around it and set the tin can of bacon grease and anise atop the stones. Light the Sterno, then hide and wait. This combo of odors is a seductive recipe.

James Matousek
Herkimer, New York

FIVE BEAR BAITING TIPS

Here are five ways to bait bears more effectively.

1. To use liquid smoke as an attractant and a cover scent, put it in a spray bottle and spray the trees around the bait site.

2. Use a liquid scent (if legal where you hunt) as part of your baiting material. Liquid scent reaches out farther through the air than solid bait. Also, after eating at a bait station and leaving, a bear will carry a liquid scent trail on its paws that other bears will find, and follow back to your bait.

3. If legal, dig a hollow stump in the ground and place your bait inside. Then place a large rock over the opening on top of the stump. This way, when the bait has been hit, you know a bear has been there. The rock will be too heavy for a raccoon, fisher or other small animal to move.

4. Place sand around the bait and rake it out after each visit. That way, you can see the track sizes of the bears that are visiting the bait.

5. When looking at tracks to determine a general size of the bear, measure the width of the front pad. A 5-inch or wider pad usually indicates a bear exceeding 300 pounds.

Marty Kamrowski
Arcadia, Wisconsin

Tracks tell the story of what kind of bear(s) are hitting your bait. According to the author, a pad wider than 5 inches means a 300-pound-plus bear.

KILL SCENT EFFECTIVELY

To kill your scent in a treestand effectively, bring a bottle of liquid smoke. After I'm up in my treestand, I shake a couple of drops all around me. It seems to kill my scent, plus it smells good.

Kate Hoppe
Powell, Wyoming

SOCKS OVER BOOTS

It might look stupid, but wearing socks over your boots will, to a degree, muffle the sound of your footsteps, especially on packed dirt trails. For added benefit, put fresh, clean socks in a zip-top bag and sprinkle them with a few drops of scent or scent-mask. Keep the bag sealed until needed.

Jed Binkly
Vancouver, Washington

TWO-BOGGAN OUT YOUR GAME

I made an inexpensive game transporter I call a "two-boggan" from two wooden toboggans. It was simple to build, and it's useful for hauling out game. Here's how.

I fastened the two toboggans together with cut lengths of old hockey sticks screwed in across the toboggans alongside their fastening straps. This provides a double-wide toboggan that works well for transporting game, especially in areas where vehicle access is restricted.

The extra width provides the space necessary to hold game in place. We brought three quarters of a young moose out in one trip last season. It only required one person to pull that load, and the effort was minimal. The second moose we brought out was in an area we had reached with ATVs. We simply tied the "two-boggan" behind the ATV and hauled the entire animal to the truck!

I secure game to the "two-boggan" using nylon rope zigzagged side to side. Another alternative is rubber bungee straps.

James R. Shewfelt
Sherwood Park, Alberta

The two-boggan.

The author appreciates his two-boggan for hauling big antlers too.

CREATE A HUNTING BICYCLE

I picked up an old 10-speed bike at a garage sale for $10, and equipped it with saddlebags and a leather rifle scabbard. The scabbard attaches to the bike frame with rubber bungee cords, and is angled so the barrel points to the rear and down, and the stock rides above the handlebars.

In areas of restricted vehicle access, this is an excellent and effective way to get around. I have harvested many birds, as well as deer, elk and moose while using my bike.

Get into a saddle—a bike saddle—to get way back-in where the game is.

One word of caution: If you use a bike to hunt big game, keep in mind how far back you've ridden. A short bicycle ride turns into a long ordeal if you shoot something and must drag it out!

James R. Shewfelt
Sherwood Park, Alberta

AMMUNITION FOR BIG GAME

All the major ammo makers supply excellent centerfire ammunition. The dilemma comes in the bullet you choose. There are flat ones, pointed ones, boattails, flat-based models, polycarbonate tips, silvertips, soft lead tips and copper alloys.

Although some guns shoot most cartridges suitably, other firearms are selective about what they like. Some rifles like light pointed bullets, and some like heavy round-nosed bullets. Only by shooting will you identify what your rifle likes.

In choosing a bullet style for a hunt, first choose the bullet grain that best suits your purpose. The next choice is bullet style. Do you want a rapidly expanding bullet that stays in the animal, or one that plows a good blood groove and exits your quarry? In choosing your ammunition, read the box, remembering that "thick-skinned dangerous game" does not include a 100-pound white-tailed deer. Knowledgeable sales staff might be able to help you.

If all else fails, talk to a gun buff or gunsmith, or do some research on the Internet. Remember, the bullet is the first part of your gear that comes in contact with your trophy. If it doesn't perform, you don't get your trophy.

When you find the brand, bullet grain and bullet style that shoots best in your rifle, do yourself a favor: Buy several boxes of that exact ammo. Be sure the lot number printed on the ammo box is identical. Trust me: They all shoot differently to some degree, and by buying identical ammo, you will save sighting-in costs each time you change ammo.

And remember to be a good sport and sight in your rifle before each hunt.

Jim Mansell
Callander, Ontario

SPOTTING SCOPE HANDLE

I needed a handle for my spotting scope that would make the unit fast and easy to use, as well as easily carried in a daypack. To craft such a handle, I cut a 3-inch chunk of wood from an old hammer handle and drilled a ¼-inch hole through the center. Then I put a ¼-inch carriage bolt with standard threads through the handle and screwed it into the spotting scope.

To use it, I grasp the handle with one hand and steady it with the other while resting my elbows on my stomach. If I'm sitting, I put my elbows on my knees. If you use a high-magnification scope, you will need to lean against a tree, stump or boulder to help steady yourself.

Randy Offenburger
Lacona, Iowa

MOOSE CALLING STRATEGIES

Here are some things I've learned over the years about moose calling.

SOFT DOES THE TRICK

If you get a response from a bull moose when using a cow call during the rut, soften the tone of the call until the bull will come no closer. If you can see the bull, walk away from him so he can see you. Try calling again, using a soft tone with the cow call. If the bull responds and continues to approach to find the cow, allow the bull to see you one more time. Then, once again walk away, conceal yourself and continue the soft call while keeping the bull in view. He should continue advancing until within shooting range.

WATCH SCENT, DON'T BE TOO AGGRESSIVE

When calling moose, remember that a bull will try to wind you when it hears the calls, because a moose's eyesight is not as good as a deer's, but its senses of smell and hearing are flawless. Lie low in a small hollow or sheltered area on the ground to control your scent. If you have a bull moose interested in your cow call, and it will not come within range, try grunting like a bull moose in a low tone so it sounds like another bull moose is nearby and infringing on his territory. Do not break branches or bang wood into branches, because this sign of aggression might scare off a moose; plus, when the rutting season arrives, the bulls' fighting stage has passed.

IMITATE A MOOSE HAREM

Imitating a cow moose when you spot a cow might lure in a bull. Bull moose collect a small harem of cows and will mate with the one that is ready, making the other cow moose jealous. If imitating a cow moose does not work, I sometimes use a short cry that mimics a calf moose. This will usually stop a cow moose long enough to get a shot.

Richard Darling
Kenora, Ontario

PICTURE-PERFECT TARGET PRACTICE

Take images of game animals from magazines and use them as targets for shooting practice. This is a great way to focus on the animal's kill zone. Your "kill zone" is a lot smaller than on the real thing, making you shoot better.

Toby Mohr
Manchester, Pennsylvania

Pictures of game from magazines and other sources (left) are great for target practice (right), helping hunters of any age have fun and learn to hold on the kill zone.

HOW TO PHOTOGRAPH YOUR TROPHIES

Always carry a good 35mm camera with zoom lens and carry several rolls of different film speeds. Try not to field dress the downed animal before all pictures have been taken. Always keep water and towels in your vehicle for washing away blood between photos. Cut the tongue out so it does not show in the photo. Before the season starts, buy a pair of taxidermy glass eyes to put over the animal's eyes so

The author's tips will help you create pleasing, tasteful photo memories of your trophy.

there will not be reflection from a flash. Take photos from several different angles, and try to skyline the antlers or horns. Try several poses and in some, stand back and hold the head an arm's length away. By following these guidelines, you'll have better photos.

Vincent Butts
Tecumseh, Michigan

PHOTOGRAPHING YOUR TROPHY

When it's time to take photos of your trophy, these tips can enhance your pictures. Put 1 to 2 feet of monofilament fishing line in your wallet, backpack, first-aid kit or survival kit. Before taking photos, clean any blood from around the animal's nose and mouth. Then take the fishing line and tie the animal's mouth shut after putting its tongue back inside the mouth. These tips really make a noticeable difference in the quality of your photo memories.

Mark Zastrow
Watertown, Wisconsin

 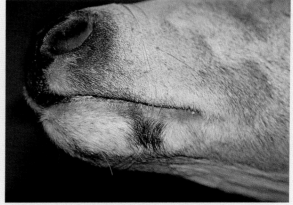

Carry a little fishing line (left) to tie an animal's mouth shut (right) at picture-taking time. No more lolling tongues to ruin an otherwise nice photo.

ANTELOPE BUCKS AT DAWN

I love bowhunting antelope in country with rolling hills, using a spot-and-stalk method. My most effective method is to be in the field at daylight and find antelope grazing on a hill's western slope.

Careful not to skyline myself, I get positioned below the hill's crest directly between the buck and the sun. By crawling slowly, I can consistently get within bow range. When stalking at daybreak, I find the animals are much more relaxed. In fact, many times they're not alarmed even if they see me. The key is to stay low and work slowly into the wind.

In one instance, I crawled about 50 yards to get within 70 yards of a buck and four does. I was sitting out in the open, and the antelope occasionally looked right at me and continued to feed in my direction. I remained still and eventually got a broadside shot at the buck at 35 yards.

As I get older, I find this tactic sure beats crawling on my belly through sagebrush in the heat of the day!

Scott Lautenschlager
Aberdeen, South Dakota

Dawn is perhaps the very best time to put the stalk on a buck antelope.

ANTELOPE SKINNING FRAME

Antelope hunts frequently occur during warm weather. If the downed animal is not skinned out immediately so it can cool, there is danger the meat will spoil. It's possible to skin an antelope that is lying on the ground, but doing so is a challenge, and dirt and grass can get on the meat.

A better method is to hang the animal for skinning. Unfortunately, in most pronghorn country, there are few trees from which to hang an animal.

My solution is to carry three 8-foot-long poles (2x2s) that can be easily assembled into a tepee-like frame from which the animal can be suspended for skinning. At one end of each pole, construct a fork by nailing, on opposite sides, two 16-inch-long, 1- by 2-inch extensions that will form a 6-inch-deep fork. The forks on each pole can then be intertwined to create a stable framework. When not in use, the three 2x2 poles can be carried atop your truck.

Charles R. Horejsi
Missoula, Montana

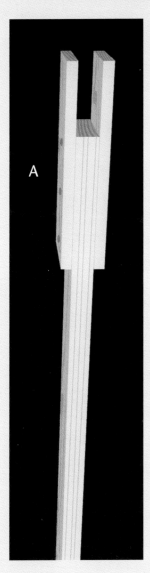

Create a fork at the end of each 2x2 pole (A), then intertwine them as the author does (B) to make a handy field tripod for skinning antelope or other game where there are no trees.

SPECIAL TIPS SECTION

SLING STOPPER

Sew a button atop the shoulder of your hunting coat to help keep your gun sling from sliding off your shoulder when walking.

Robert J. Manske
Portage, Wisconsin

A simple button will hold your gun sling where you want it.

TAGGING BIG GAME

When it is necessary to tag big game through the ear, use a large safety pin. This makes a smaller hole than cutting with a knife, and it still secures the tag. You can also use the pins for emergency repairs.

Robert G. Floyd
Conestoga, Pennsylvania

TRY A HANDGUN BIPOD

For those of us who hunt with big-bore handguns, holding the gun steady is sometimes difficult. The obvious answer is to use some sort of rest for the gun. I prefer a bipod. The problem is, you can't attach a bipod to the gun and still holster it for transport. One solution: Use hard plastic, spring-loaded bipods. They fit easily into a cargo pocket of your pants and are designed to fit any size barrel. In a matter of two or three seconds, you can mount the bipod to your gun for a steady shot. The best part is that these bipods are inexpensive, sometimes costing less than $10.

Dan Blackwell
Canon City, Colorado

CLEANING MOUNTS

To clean trophy mounts, use canned air that you buy for cleaning your computer. This works great. It gets the dust out of the tightest places without damage.

Robert J. Manske
Portage, Wisconsin

Air out your mounts and they'll last longer.

EASY HAULING

For hauling out your downed big game, try an old-fashioned toboggan, your child's snow sled or a calf sled—a device used by cattlemen for pulling newborn calves into shelter. These items will make the drag much easier while saving time and energy. I have used a sled for elk, and it works wonders.

John Paczkowski
Bismarck, North Dakota

WHEELED TUB FOR GEAR TRANSPORT

Whenever I'm setting up base camp in an automobile-accessible area, I use a heavy-duty plastic 45-gallon storage tub with wheels to store my gear. I can fit my sleeping bag, tent, tarp, raincoat, spare clothes, canteen, ammo, toiletries and extra rations inside. A domed lid helps shed rain; wheels and side handles make the tub easy to load in and out of a pickup.

Various fastening hardware can be installed on the sides to serve as tie-down anchors for bungee cords, which can be used to attach things such as a folding chair, fishing rod or camp stove. This is an excellent way to keep your gear in one place and prevent it from getting mixed up with your buddy's stuff.

Jed Binkly
Vancouver, Washington

PROTECT YOUR BARREL

Here's a tip that works well: Cut one of the fingers off a latex glove and put it over the end of your gun barrel to keep rain and snow out of the barrel. There is no need to take it off before the shot, because it does not affect accuracy.

Eric Houser
Southgate, Michigan

Cut off the fingertip of a latex glove and slide it over your barrel during inclement weather.

UNSCENTED BABY WIPES

My husband and I never leave home without unscented baby wipes. They're handy for use in the camper or in the truck after loading up our game. We also carry loose ones in zip-top baggies in our backpacks.

Kate Hoppe
Powell, Wyoming

TRAILING GAME

When tracking wounded game through ferns, use the back of your hand in an upward sweeping motion to check for blood on the underside of fern leaves. When deer and other big game go through ferns, blood often ends up on the underside. Once the animal has passed through, the ferns drop back to their downward position.

John Straight
Oregon City, Oregon

"CAMO" FOR PRONGHORNS

The best camouflage for hunting pronghorn antelope is a pair of faded blue jeans and a faded brown shirt. These blend in with the sagebrush and dry grass better than any commercially made camo clothes. Hunters wearing some of the commercial camo stand out like a lump of coal on a snowbank.

Bill Stewart
Douglas, Wyoming

FOAMING SPRAY FOR TRACKING

Hydrogen peroxide in a spray bottle can be sprayed on the ground and plants to find small blood spots. This common liquid foams when it hits blood.

John Straight
Oregon City, Oregon

QUICK CLEANUP

Carry some wet wipes to clean up after field dressing game. This makes quick work of removing blood, dirt and so on.

Robert G. Floyd
Conestoga,
Pennsylvania

Wet wipes are perfect for in-the-field cleanup needs.

STEAM FLETCHING BACK TO LIFE

Here's a tip that might prove useful to bowhunters who use feathers instead of vanes. Hunting in damp conditions in Alaska is almost unavoidable. Because I'm a traditional bowhunter, shooting off the shelf requires me to use feathers on my arrows. Regardless of how hard I try, feathers get crushed, matted, wet and otherwise distorted.

Steam your feathers back into shape, let them dry overnight, then waterproof them again.

These problems are easily fixed with a teakettle of boiling water. Slowly rotate the feathers in the steam to gently correct the feather, and your fletches will return to their original condition in just a few minutes. Let them dry overnight and then re-treat them with your waterproofing of choice. I like to use Kiwi Camp Dry. I hope this helps other members of the Club. Keep your broadheads sharp and the wind in your face.

Martin Farris
Chugiak, Alaska

Adventure

Hunting adventures can be big and expensive. But they can also be small and affordable.

What matters in an adventure is how much you anticipate the hunt before it happens, how well you prepare for it, how hard you hunt while you're at it ... and how good it makes you feel to have done it.

Here are some adventures and tips to inspire you on to your own forays.

ARE HUNTERS RECRUITING ANTI-HUNTERS?

Once considered a necessary, accepted way of life, hunting is now a political hot potato. We finally got the deer off the car fenders in many parts of the country, but now it's time to further clean up our image.

I recently traveled to hunt in Montana. While flying from Richmond, Virginia, to Detroit and then to Minneapolis, I appeared to be the only hunter on the aircraft. After changing planes for the flight from Minneapolis to Bozeman, it seemed more than half the passengers were hunters. How did I know? Easy. Most were wearing some part of a camouflage outfit. Some wore their outfits proudly. Others looked like military rejects or escapees from Fort Leavenworth prison. The most interesting were those with camo shirts open to their belly buttons to reveal three or four gold chains. It seems to me we have a duty to look and act professionally. We are the image many people form of all hunters.

TAKE BETTER PICTURES

When taking pictures of hunters with their trophies, always clean up the blood as much as possible. Position the animal so that you can't see the bullet or arrow hole. Make sure the animal's tongue is in its mouth. The person taking the picture should have the sun at his back or come in from one side, and try getting low to the ground for a couple of pictures. Have the hunter and the game in front of a good backdrop, such as trees, water or mountains. If possible, set up on a hill with the sky for a background, and have the hunter hold the animal's head to the side where the antlers will make a nice skyline picture. Always take lots of pictures. Film is a cheap but valuable investment for your trophy.

John D. Fallon
Doylestown, Pennsylvania

The other group of hunters was also noticeable. They wore their big boots, and kept sticking them into the aisles for flight attendants to trip over. Still others stood up most of the flight and talked loudly so all could see and hear.

Interestingly, on the return flight, most of the same people were there. For the most part, though, they were dressed casually and were quiet and kept to themselves. Why didn't they behave that way going out?

On the flight out, I dressed casually, knowing I had a day and a half to relax and sightsee. Sitting to my right was a self-employed computer whiz kid from Detroit who was going to visit his girlfriend. To my left was a grandmother from Baltimore going to visit her son, a university professor in Bozeman.

The first 45 minutes were basically quiet, but then the "hunters" got a burst of arrogance. The noise level rose, with the hunters talking as if they were about to engage in guerilla warfare on animals. The computer guy asked, "Don't those people have to pass a test or something to hunt?"

I replied, "I don't think so."

"A shame," he replied. "They probably wouldn't be here if they had to."

The noise level grew louder. I noted 12 individuals standing and shouting to each other over the other passengers. The one behind us with the four gold chains slapped the back of our seat and laughed, raising his hands to the ceiling and shouting: "I'm going to shoot him again and again. This is my second year. No more waiting. This year if I see it, I'm going to kill it."

With that, another gold-chain man clad in camo raised his cap and proclaimed, "I'm going to kill, kill, kill." Another man with a camo cap stood and joined in. What a bad impression, even to seasoned hunters.

I then noticed five teenaged girls, all watching and listening earnestly. I was too afraid to ask what they were learning.

Meanwhile, my seatmates asked a few more

questions, including what I do for a living. I said that I'm a part-time consultant and freelance writer. The computer guy asked, "What kind of writing do you do?"

"I write about God," I replied. "And His creatures, conservation and the balance of nature. You know, helping keep God's creations in harmony. I do some research first. That's why I'm going to Montana. To do research for some articles. I'm going up into the mountains on a hunting and fishing adventure."

Silence. It lasted about three or four minutes, and then the grandmother asked, "What do you do with the animals?" From that point on, we talked about recipes and cooking tips.

The computer guy then said, "I just can't get into hunting."

He said he visited Montana every month. I asked if he had seen animals in town in the winter, and dead along the roadside from accidents or starvation. He said he had, and I replied, "That's one way of balancing nature, but it's painful and often very slow."

Much has been written about hunter ethics, safety, sportsmanship and landowner rights. Now it's time to look in the mirror. Who and what do we represent and how?

A smile goes a long way. Courtesy and first impressions are persuasive. Save the arrogance, stories, bragging, gold chains and "kill" stories for camp. When in public, be a good representative of your peers. Be a true conservationist. Conserve the sport.

John Caknipe
Chase City, Virginia

KEEP A DIARY

I keep a hunting diary on all of my hunting trips, along with the map of the area I'm hunting. When hunting in the same area the next trip or year, I know how far it is to our campsite, how long it takes to get there, things I don't want to forget the next time, what the weather was like, and so on.

I also write down the names of new hunting friends and game wardens who stop by camp, and what kind of vehicles they were driving. I reread my diary before I go back, and it is just like yesterday, only usually a year later. People are amazed I remember their names a year later.

Kate Hoppe
Powell, Wyoming

The author's field diary helps her get beautiful, tall-horned pronghorn bucks like this.

SPOT MORE GAME

Why is it that some hunters see more game than others? What makes them able to find game when others cannot? Let's look at some of the factors.

To start, it's essential to believe game is present. Even when there is no sign of game, you must keep a positive attitude or you will find only exit tracks as proof that a buck or bull saw you first. No matter how long you go without seeing sign, keep a positive attitude and you will see more game. Check out anything that looks different. Determine what caused your curiosity. Many hunters can tell

Rare indeed is the clear view of an entire game animal. This muley buck is easily looked past.

you about a stump that had not been there earlier in the day.

Second, use all of your senses. If it were not for our ability to think, humans would be extinct. Our senses are poor compared to many other species'.

We do not see like an eagle, hear like a mule deer, or decipher scents like an elk. To position ourselves to find and see game, we must use all of our senses.

Think about the times you've seen game. What was your first indication that game was present? Chances are, you heard it first. Also, don't overlook your sense of smell. Elk leave an odor even humans can detect. I have even smelled a rutting buck before I saw or heard him.

Third, take mental pictures. What do you envision when you think of deer? Do you see the whole deer or just a head with enormous antlers? You will improve your ability to spot game if you build mental pictures of game, their colors and parts at various angles, sizes and distances. What does a mule deer's ear look like at 50 yards? What does an elk look like at 400 yards on a brushy hillside, or a whitetail's leg look like under a tree?

In most cases, it pays to think small when looking for game. Most people overestimate the size of the game and, consequently, they look for something large. At great distances, deer get small quickly. Whole animals can be visible at distances, but because we look for something larger, we sometimes don't correlate what we see as an animal.

Practice can help, both in the wild and by using life-sized replicas. Place a life-sized replica at a known distance and look at it, then change its position, distance and angle. Use your binoculars too. You would be surprised how many hunters think binoculars make game look huge and, consequently, bypass game because they think their binoculars should be filled with the animal.

Always look for parts of a deer. The first thing you see on a deer will likely be an ear, a rump, a leg or an antler. Again, the hunter's brain is a hindrance. When we hunt, we tend to look for a whole deer, not part of a deer. But seldom will you see the whole animal, even under the best conditions.

Be sure to "amplify" differences you detect in the landscape. I spot a lot of game simply because at first glance I noticed something was "different." Something was out of place or unusual. It might be a color difference or a vertical or horizontal line that seemed out of place.

When hunting with a partner, be able to quickly describe locations. If you see something and tell your partner, you might have just seconds to help him locate the buck of a lifetime. First, tell him there is something you need him to verify. Next, use the time-target method to describe a spot. Pick a clearly identifiable object both of you see and imagine it as the center of a target. Then locate a distant object and call it the "10 circle" or outer circle of a target. Now describe the buck's location as, for example, "the 5 circle at 2 o'clock." In other words, combine a target with the clock. This technique also works when you need to relocate game you spotted earlier.

Lanny D. Olson
Puyallup, Washington

PLAY IT COOL

When still-hunting, if a game animal spots you before or at the same time you spot it, do not stop to look. Do not make eye contact or crouch down to get a better look with binoculars. Predators crouch, and you don't want your quarry to think of you as its predator.

It's best to continue at the same pace while angling gradually away. This will give the animal the impression you never saw it, and it will have no reason to leave. Most likely, it will stay put, giving you a chance to get a better look once you have found a good barrier between you and the animal.

Too many hunters in this situation immediately stop, drop down and pull out the binoculars. These actions—except the part about the binoculars—are the same as a four-legged predator's, and the prey animal will not usually stick around to find out what will happen, especially the bigger bucks and bulls that know the game of survival all too well and wear the headgear to prove it.

Eric Torgerson
Rigby, Idaho

GO UP ONE SIZE IN PAC BOOTS

When you buy felt-lined pac boots, buy them at least one size larger than what you normally wear. This allows for a couple of things. First, it gives you room to wear an extra pair of socks. Second, it allows you to put a pair of felt insoles inside the felt pacs. Most cold feet are the result of standing still, and the cold is transmitted to the feet from the ground. Those extra insoles make all the difference in the world and can mean the difference between enjoying the hunt and suffering with cold feet.

James R. Shewfelt
Sherwood Park, Alberta

DEALING WITH BEAVERS

We have a large beaver population in central Saskatchewan. These large furbearers are very adept at flooding fields and destroying pastures. To control these animals, unless bound by regulation, leave the .22-caliber rifle at home. A .223 is about as small as you can go to consistently make one-shot kills. Most shots will be fired in low-light conditions, but with plenty of contrast during sunrise and sunset.

If beavers have had no hunting pressure in the past three or so years, they will be active all day. Once they're experienced, though, they will move only at dawn and dusk. When hunting beavers, sneak in and be ready for action. If you only hear their loud warning splash, watch carefully. The beaver will be back within 30 seconds to keep an eye on you. A beaver can stick his nose and eyes above the surface without breaking a ripple. If you don't see anything, throw something in the water to make some waves. If you still see nothing, rip a large hole in the dam and wait. They will come to investigate.

Camouflage is not as important as being still. You must be sure never to get skylined. If suitable trees are available, treestands have proven effective.

It is time-consuming but not difficult to keep beavers from being active. Hunt every day until they stop rebuilding their dams. Then hunt once a week to keep them from returning. No beavers means ponds can drain. Explosives help destroy dams, but are usually only needed for old, grown-in dams.

Hunting beavers is great fun and a challenge because they remain well suited to their watery home. Whether you try shooting them in the water is your choice, but be aware that ricochets are highly possible when firing into water, so know your surroundings and be safety conscious. Utilize the pelts for a few extra dollars.

Karl Abrahamson
Pelly, Saskatchewan

STUDY BEFORE YOU LEAVE HOME

When planning a trip for trophy caribou in Quebec or any other destination—which is likely to be a once-in-a-lifetime experience—take the time to do what I call "in-home scouting." Rent a couple of caribou hunting videos. They will usually show a good number of caribou in a herd, which allows you to see many sizes of antlers so you can compare and determine what is a good bull. When you are used to hunting whitetails in eastern Pennsylvania, as I am, even small-antlered caribou look huge! So take the time to study pictures, magazines and videos before leaving for your trip. Once there, don't shoot the first animal you see, because there are some great bulls up there.

The author learned what a truly big bull looked like ... and then brought one home.

I arrived in Quebec on a Sunday, and I took my first bull on Tuesday after passing up several caribou. After passing on several more bulls, it wasn't till Thursday that I took a larger bull, a beautiful record-book caribou. That was the most exciting moment I've ever had afield. That bull scored 392⅜, and I am very proud of my trophy.

John D. Sheaffer
Adamstown, Pennsylvania

THE GATOR

DESIRE, RESEARCH & PERSISTENCE CAN HELP YOU GET THERE

It took us seven years of accumulating preference points to get drawn for our first alligator hunt. Jack Harmeyer and I were excited when we found out we would be hunting the J. D. Murphy Wildlife Management Area (WMA) in Texas. We called biologists, reviewed studies, photographed alligators at a state park, talked to outfitters and read everything we could about big alligators.

The week before the hunt, we paid special attention to our baits, starting out with freshly dressed whole chickens and marinating them for three days outdoors in the South Texas heat. We checked all the knots on our rigs and sharpened our 12/0 hooks with a fine honing stone.

The hunt started in the afternoon, and we motored our rental boat through a series of levees to our assigned area. We proceeded to scout. Figuring that big gators would hang out in big holes, we hung our bait over the largest, deepest hole we could find. Sure enough, we had an alligator hooked the next morning. With Jack pulling the gator to the surface hand over hand, I missed the first shot. After the gator quit splashing and rolling, I shot again and he went belly up. We pulled him half out of the water, tied his mouth shut and, after much heaving, got him into the boat. Fortunately, Jack tied both ends of the big gator to the boat while I tagged him.

Somewhere on the way back, we realized this gator wasn't dead. A closer look revealed the slug had bounced off the skull as if it were a slab of concrete. Jack straddled the saurian and stuck him behind the skull with his 3-inch Swiss army knife. The reptile repeatedly heaved sideways violently, almost capsizing the boat, and then finally went limp. With a sigh of relief, Jack proclaimed, "I felt just like I was McGyver Dundee."

You could fill a book with tips on how to navigate the swamp in the dark with a blown boat engine, how to fend off formations of mosquitoes, how to avoid falling into the drink and how to avoid scraping yourself with a hook covered in rotten chicken. The best tip is that gator hunting sure is fun!

Paul Beachy
Colorado Springs, Colorado

DETAILS ON THE GATOR

Who:	Jack Harmeyer and Paul Beachy
What:	American alligator, "Booger"
When:	Early fall alligator season
Where:	J. D. Murphy WMA on the Gulf Coast of Mexico in Jefferson County, Texas
How:	With bait, hook, line and Calcutta pole. Shot with Remington pump-action 20 gauge and slugs
How big:	11-foot 1-inch bull alligator, weighing 320 pounds; largest alligator killed on the WMA that year

They named him "Booger."

 # SPECIAL TIPS SECTION

HANDY EMERGENCY SIGNAL

If you need an emergency signal whistle, use an empty centerfire rifle cartridge. Place the open end on your lower lip with the cartridge in a vertical position and blow air down into the cartridge. With practice, you can produce a whistle that can be heard for 1 to 1½ miles.

Gregory Gilpin
Mount Pleasant, Pennsylvania

An empty centerfire rifle cartridge makes a loud and clear emergency whistle.

MAKING EMERGENCY FIRE-STARTERS

To make an emergency fire-starter, take a cupcake tin made for small cupcakes. Melt paraffin wax in a pan and mix it with sawdust. Pour the mixture into the cupcake mold and place the tin in cold water. Pop out the "cake" and carry it with you in a sealed zip-top bag.

Mike Weiss
Reese, Michigan

Create emergency fire-starter "cakes" using paraffin wax and sawdust.

CHEAP FIRE-STARTER

For a cheap fire-starter, consider using a rinsed tuna can. Cut a strip of cardboard that's as wide as the can is deep, roll up the cardboard until it fills the can, then pour melted wax into the can until filled. To use the fire-starter, gouge the cardboard a little to form a small wick, then light it.

Mike Moore
Lincoln, Nebraska

SPECIAL SECTION
ADVENTURE TIPS

KEEP AMMO FRESH

To keep your ammunition fresh and untarnished—especially rounds you don't use very often—wrap the ammo box twice with heavy aluminum foil, sealing it well. Store in a dark, cool, dry place.

William Tong
Lufkin, Texas

Wrap a box of ammunition in tinfoil to keep the cartridges fresh and untarnished.

ARCHERY TARGET

On a hunting trip about 10 years ago, we forgot our archery target, so I stuffed my polyfiber pillow (without case), into a box. It stopped every arrow, even carbon. Since then all I shoot at is three polyfiber pillows inside a box. Every once in a while, I pack it down or replace the box. I like to practice with broadheads, and the pillows are excellent for stopping them. Some broadheads are hard to remove. Fibers catch on their back side upon removal. Muzzy has practice blades for some of their models, which don't catch on removal. I haven't bought a new target in 10 years.

Harvey Surprenant
Chitek Lake, Saskatchewan

KEEP FIREARMS SAFE

All gun owners must do more to protect their valuable firearms. I suggest the following in case your firearms ever become lost, destroyed or stolen.

- Write down all serial numbers, model numbers and calibers.
- Take photos of each firearm and note important numbers on the back of each photo.
- Place the photos and descriptions in a safe place that is fireproof, such as a safe-deposit box.
- Write your name, address and telephone number on a piece of paper. Place this paper under the butt plate of all guns. Do the same on handgun grips.

Michael D. Winkel
Marshfield, Wisconsin

VACUUM-PACK IT ALL

Last year I went on a caribou hunting trip to Alaska. It was a drop-hunt, which meant living out of a tent. I knew it would be wet at times, so I used a Food Saver Vacuum Packaging System to vacuum-pack my clothing individually. It was easy to pack, and I did not have to worry about anything getting wet until I opened the bag. I also used the vacuum packs for individual meals, which I could eat right out of the bags cold, or after boiling the food right in the bag.

Dean Zink
Wisconsin Dells, Wisconsin

Packing is easy—and everything stays dry—when you seal it up tight in a vacuum pack.

WASH CLOTHES INSIDE OUT

To keep your camouflage clothing from fading because of continuous washing—sometimes we must wash even our lucky shirt—turn it inside out before washing. Also, fasten all closures, buttons, zippers, Velcro or whatever. Then put them into the washer. This helps the colors stay longer.

George Walker
Mansfield, Texas

FEATHER REVEALS WIND DIRECTION

Tie a feather to one end of a string and then tie the other end of the string to the end of your gun barrel. With the feather hanging below the barrel, you will always know the wind's direction, which helps you stay downwind of game you're hunting.

Chris Kerr
McKinney, Texas

SIGHT IN EASILY

When sighting in guns, use a spotting scope and two targets to save trips back and forth taping holes. Tape one target in place on the range, and keep the other by your side. Now, shoot at the range target and, using your scope, mark the hit on the other target. Tracking your hits will never be easier!

Robert J. Manske
Portage, Wisconsin

To save trips back and forth to the target, keep a second target near your spotting scope. Mark the downrange hits on this target as you map out your sighting-in progress.

SNAP SUSPENDER CLIP INTO BELT LOOP

To help keep your suspenders from slipping off your pants, hook the clip into the belt loop. The belt loop has double thickness at the top, and the clip will not slip off.

Richard D. Haines
Columbia, Pennsylvania

BARREL RAIN PROTECTION

Put a piece of Scotch tape over the end of your rifle or shotgun barrel to keep out rain, snow, dirt and debris. It's cheap, quick and effective.

Joe Rode
Traverse City, Michigan

CHEAP, EFFECTIVE FIRE-STARTER

I've discovered a cheap, effective fire-starter. First, take a cottonball and coat its fibers with Vaseline, then put it in a 35mm film canister. Keep doing this until the canister is full. When you need a quick fire, pull out a wadded up cotton ball or two, and pull the fibers apart gently to allow air to circulate. Light it with a match or lighter, and it will burn for about 90 seconds, which is plenty of time to get a good fire going.

Chad Goeden
Ninilchik, Alaska

Coat cotton-ball fibers with Vaseline (top) to make some great fire-starters (bottom).

GUNSMITHING

Iron sights that fit into dovetail slots in a gun barrel are always driven right to left, so they must be driven out from left to right. The slot is tapered to create a tight fit.

James Matousek
Herkimer, New York

Iron sights are driven right to left, removed left to right.

BLACK MARKER CAMOUFLAGE

Use a black marker to cover the shiny items of your hunting gear. For example, most broadheads are shiny. I color them with a marker to eliminate glare.

Chris Hausher
Oologah, Oklahoma

A heavy-duty black marker eliminates shine.

Making Matches Waterproof

To make waterproof matches for your pack, take an empty shotgun shell, insert wooden kitchen matches, refold the case mouth and drip candle wax on the crimp end. Now you have waterproof matches for your next hunting trip.

Mike Weiss
Reese, Michigan

To create a waterproof match compartment (left), you need matches, a spent shotshell and wax (right). Put the matches in the shell, crimp it closed and seal shut with melted wax.

Rifle Sling Stopper

Pin a round-ball compass on the shoulder of your hunting jacket. This prevents your rifle sling from slipping down the side of your arm.

Richard Boliver
Croghan, New York

GAME BIRDS

Bird hunting offers unique rewards.

Making a good shot at a bird on the wing has to be one of the most satisfying accomplishments known to humankind. The special bond formed between hunter and dog also creates lifelong memories.

See what NAHC Members have to say about the art of hunting our beautiful and elusive game birds.

WHEN ONE BUCK WAS WORTH
MORE THAN A MILLION DOLLARS

Today, $125 might seem like a lot of money, but to a 13-year-old in 1983, it seemed more like $1 million. I had that money saved up, and I wanted just one thing: a dog. Wanting a dog is simple enough, right? Except I wanted a bird dog. So with all the charm a young, potential hunter could possess, I begged and promised all sorts of things, and Mom and Dad agreed.

One stipulation was that a kennel be built first. And Mom held me to it. Chicken wire, cedar poles and some of Grandpa's rough-sawn lumber solved the problem but brought about another: Where would I find a pup? The answer came where one might expect it: the local paper—but not in the want ads.

The paper ran a picture of "Babe," a golden retriever bitch that whelped 11 pups. A phone call and a visit to the owners secured me one of those pups. Picking him was easy. I chose the darkest red one, which just happened to be the runt of the litter. The purchase price was 125 bucks, which helped inspire the pup's very original name, "Buck."

Buck too was a dark red golden retriever. He grew old while the author grew up.

Never having trained a dog, I needed Ma to come to the rescue again. She checked out a copy of Richard Wolter's *Gun Dog* from the library. Buck's training took place on the front lawn. His reward for good work was a chunk of hot dog and a lot of petting. Punishment was almost nonexistent.

Bird season came fast, and I was ready. I admit I wouldn't have known if I was really ready, because I had never hunted birds before. I did know, though, that a partridge was a grouse! Being a country boy, I needed only to walk out of the house and into the woods. I borrowed Dad's 20 gauge Mossberg bolt, called out my half-grown pup, and became a bird hunter.

The "Peak" is a big hill I can look at through the front window of my current "kennel," and it was the cover I chose that first opening day. My only other transportation modes (besides shoe leather) were a Yamaha three-wheeler and a garden tractor trailer for Bucky to ride in. While walking into a clear-cut, Buck flushed the first bird we ever encountered and I made the shot! There never was a prouder hunter than I when Buck retrieved that first bird.

The Peak is a place I consider sacred because, in addition to that first bird, it also produced my first white-tailed deer and my first black bear.

That first year, Buck and I logged more miles together than I ever have in a single season since.

Rarely did we run into anyone. Once, while hunting the "swamp," I heard a truck coming. I had two birds in hand (I always had to carry them because I didn't have a hunting vest). There came the truck—a new Suburban—with a hunter driving and two pointers riding shotgun. The hunter had the best of everything: a beautiful truck, two dogs and even a vest.

He also had the best of intentions when he stopped and said, "You're having a good day, kid." He had not been lucky himself that day. Looking back, I realize Buck and I must have been a sight: skinny kid, old gun, half-grown pup and that old three-wheeler and trailer a couple of miles down the road.

Little did that hunter know that we crossed paths on my best day of the year. I missed a lot of shots that season, but Buck always found the birds. If that hunter is out there somewhere, I want to thank him for the praise.

The next four years, I was in high school. When September rolled around, Buck and I would start roaming. We became better hunters. I learned how to shoot and what a "birdy" dog looked like. When college called, I went, leaving Buck home with Mom and Dad. It was a busy time in my life, but I always made it home for the bird openers and on weekends so Buck and I could hunt together.

One weekend, I noticed Buck was stumbling when he jumped out of my truck. I knew something was wrong. The veterinarian confirmed he had Lyme disease. At the time, I was a broke college kid, but Dad came through and paid for the treatment. Though Buck got better, the disease slowed him down. We still hunted many years after, because it would have killed Buck for sure if we couldn't hunt.

A few years after getting married, I bought the house I grew up in. By then, my parents lived just a quarter mile up the road in my great-grandfather's old house. When Buck saw me moving in just down the road, he came back to my house and stayed, although he still visited my parents every day. He would cut back and forth through our neighbor's field. You could always tell he was coming by the jingle of his accumulated dog tags, rabies vaccination tags and identification tags clipped to his collar. When the snow came that winter, Buck, at age 10, kept out of the deep snow in the field and took the road to visit. Inevitably, he was hit and killed by a car. The whole family cried the day Buck died. The last link to my childhood died too.

Shortly after I lost Buck, I hopped out of my truck one day, keys in hand. The jump caused my keys to jingle just like Buck's dog tags used to jingle. Without thinking, I turned to pet him just like I always did when he ran up to me. I turned a full circle before remembering he wasn't there anymore.

I still have a tail feather from the first bird, a picture of Buck and me, and the collar he used to wear. And reserved with those things is a special place in my heart for my first bird dog.

After the accident, I vowed to never train another bird dog. I kept that vow for all of six months. One day I came home from work and my wife said, "Go to Ironwood and pick your dog out." I did. Now I have two Labradors: Harley, who's 6 years old, and Tracker, who's 2 years old.

My wife made a good call when she gave me permission not to grow up. I'm 30 years old. My three girls say that's pretty old. But come September, I'll be bird-dogging once again. And when my kids see me acting excited as a kid at Christmas, they might look at me and think, "Dad's not that old." That's because I'll feel like a kid again—30 years old and going on 13.

Loren LaPointe
Bayfield, Wisconsin

UNTIPPABLE DOG BOWL

An angel food cake pan makes an untippable drinking bowl for a dog when you drive a stake into the ground through the hole in the pan's center.

James Matousek
Herkimer, New York

HOMEMADE RECYCLED DECOYS

Every household has white bleach, vinegar or, in my case, chain oil jugs. Collect the empty jugs to make your own decoys. Wear eye protection and use a utility knife to cut a line around the jug's handle. Discard the handle portion. From scrap pieces of ⅜-inch plywood or old paneling, cut silhouette sentinel and feeder heads with enough length so the bottom can be used as a stake. Now cut slots at various angles in the jugs. This way, there will always be heads showing, no matter which direction the geese come from.

If your jugs are all similar, they will stack well and be lightweight. Paint the heads white and the wing tips black on the jugs, and you now have snow goose filler decoys. I have more than 500 of these, and have killed many snows over them. This is an excellent between-seasons project. The biggest problem is getting enough of the proper jugs. I suggest plastics recycling industries.

The same thing can be done with 5-gallon pails for larger decoys. These pails are available from road construction crews or anywhere you can buy bulk oil. I also suggest bakeries, because they buy jams and fillers in bulk. Paint the buckets in desired color schemes. Once you decoy geese over these rigs, they're rewarding in their own right.

Anthony Roelens
Endeavour, Saskatchewan

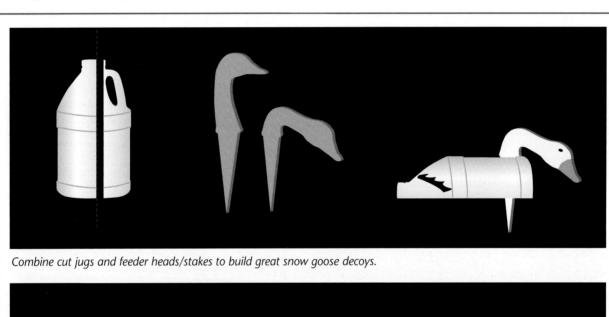

Combine cut jugs and feeder heads/stakes to build great snow goose decoys.

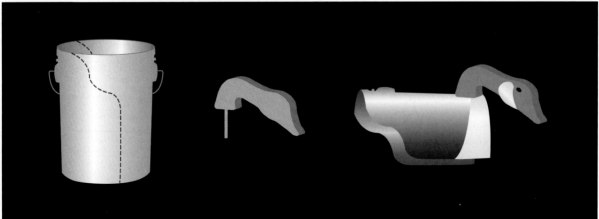

Cut 5-gallon pails and combine with a stakes/heads to make jumbo goose decoys.

HUNT WITH SHOOTING GLASSES

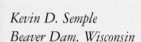

I have been trapshooting competitively for about 25 years. The sport has benefited from many improvements over the years, but one of the greatest improvements has been in shooting glasses.

A wide variety of glasses are on the market, and they come in many different colors and shades of those colors. Originally, I only wore shooting glasses while trapshooting, but it occurred to me that because the "target orange lens" greatly improved the brightness and visibility of orange clay targets, it would also improve the visibility of hunter orange clothing. Therefore, I started wearing my trapshooting glasses while deer hunting, greatly improving the visibility of other hunters I occasionally encounter in the dense, dark woods of northern Wisconsin where I hunt.

I've noticed another benefit of wearing these shooting glasses while hunting. The visibility of

See more game, protect your eyes.

game has also greatly improved! The glasses are especially helpful in hunting ruffed grouse in the thick black-alder creekbottoms we encounter in northern Wisconsin.

Not only do these glasses improve my vision, but they also protect my eyes from twigs and branches. One year I had to take one of our deer hunting crew members to the hospital because a stick injured his eye. I bet he wished he had been wearing eye protection!

The lens I like best is the lightest shade of target orange that has the "blue-blocker" feature, which greatly improves even 20/20 vision.

I do not go into the woods without shooting glasses. You shouldn't either!

Kevin D. Semple
Beaver Dam, Wisconsin

AVOID HEAVY-DUTY "TRAP" LOADS

My friend and I were out small game hunting. We weren't having too much luck, so we decided to shoot some clay pigeons. We set up the shooter and got out the clay pigeons. We decided to use my shells with his ultralight single-shot 12 gauge.

I ran into the house, grabbed a box of shells and ran back out. Because the shells were mine, my friend let me do the honors of taking the first shot. He pulled the string and the clay pigeon went flying. When I pulled the trigger, I nearly fell to the ground. My friend decided he wasn't going to try, because he's a lot smaller than I am. Nevertheless, I shot about eight or

nine more shells and called it quits because my shoulder was killing me. We started cleaning up the shells and putting the stuff away. Suddenly, my friend started laughing, and I asked what was so funny. He handed me the shell box.

I couldn't decide whether to laugh or cry. I had been shooting my box of turkey loads! I awoke the next day with a bruise on my shoulder the size of an apple. I guess the moral of the story is to always check the box before hunting or practicing!

Perry J. Ekas, age 15
Cabot, Pennsylvania

Formula for a Successful Pheasant Club

If you want a successful plan for developing a pheasant hunting club, try this formula:

Plans

1. Organize up to 36 interested people (for future club members). Put any others wanting to join on a waiting list.

2. Hold no money-making events for the club. Rely solely on annual dues.

   • Regular dues: $180; Retired dues: $140.

   • Two work days (credit): Regular: $40 for each day; Retired: $20 for each day.

3. Find an area with natural habitat for pheasants. Eventually create new habitat and increase existing habitat.

4. Hold a meeting with all members to set up club bylaws, times to meet, where to meet, and so on. Have this all done and agreed upon before meeting formally with landowners. (This is important!)

5. Organize cooperating landowners who are willing to work with you.

6. Find one landowner who will allow you to use some space for the rearing pens. The landowner might even be interested in rearing the birds for pay.

A pheasant club provides hunting access—and memorable days afield—for members willing to pay-and-work their way in.

7. Study regulations and guidelines regarding the rearing of the birds including, but not limited to, state regulations, yard, brooders and feed. **Note:** Your state department of natural resources and local feed store are good places to start.

NOTEWORTHY

One exciting thing about this program is having a trickle release, which means releasing birds three times a week. That way you'll have birds out there all the time. This ensures there will always be good hunting, and members can go out any time and experience a lot less hunting pressure in the field.

EXPLANATIONS

To make this work:

1. Organize up to 36 people. The reason for 36 or fewer members is:

   • You can get the best insurance.

   • You will not overload your hunting areas.

   • You will get much more cooperation from the landowners if they know there are 36, not 200, people on their land.

2. Make three waiting lists after you have a full membership. (My club had a 10-year waiting list.) The lists include:

   • Landowners and families, first list.

   • Members' families, second list.

   • Open membership, third list.

   Note: An existing member should sponsor each new member. Definition of a membership: One membership in a family will cover spouse and children through schooling years.

CONCLUSION

My brother Fred and I put our heads together and came up with this unique idea. Ours is a happy, successful club. Work is kept to a minimum, and the costs are affordable. Members take pride, and keep involved, in club activities, which keeps up the club's strength. Jed, our secretary/treasurer, keeps the books and records up to date so we can stay on top of everything.

We have monthly meetings. They are usually short, but the socializing is great. We talk about the exciting times we have had in the field.

I have had the pens on my property for more than 30 years, and I'm one of the landowners, so I can say, "I did it, and it's working!"

Bill Koehne
Little Suamico, Wisconsin

CHOKE TUBE HOLDERS

Use old pill bottles to hold extra choke tubes. The bottles are great for sealing out moisture and dirt. They also keep threads from getting dinged up. You can label them so you know at a glance which choke you have. The best thing, however, is if you drop the bottle into the water, it will float!

Jason Belyea
Wakefield, Nebraska

MOTION STAKES FOR SHELL DECOYS

I was not happy with the metal stakes that came with my field-type stackable shell decoys. The stakes were awkward. They often broke at the joint. They shined in the sun. They generally looked phony. So I came up with these motion stakes (page 133) to add a degree of realism to my spread.

The elastic keeps the decoy from blowing off the legs or spinning all the way around in the wind. They impart a waddling motion as they arrest the spin and rebound. The decoy also tips up and down on the fulcrum in a feeding motion. It takes little wind to get it going.

The stake and feet combination creates a stable platform, yet takes only slightly longer to set up than the metal stakes. If you need a compact package, take all of the pieces apart for transport. If not, glue some or all of the components together to ease setup. I made these rigs several seasons ago, and I am very pleased with the way they worked out.

David Sidley
Rossland, British Columbia

Finished decoys.

DECOY SAVINGS

A cost-saving way to increase your snow goose spread is to buy bulk unpainted windsock decoys. Buying in bulk saves you at least $5 or more per dozen. You will need to buy at least five dozen to get the discount. Then all you need is a can of flat black spray paint. Make a cardboard stencil for the wing patches.

My brother and I did this a few years ago, and the windsocks turned out great. We laid out the windsocks and spray-painted the stencil and the eyes. After a couple of hours' drying time, our spread was complete. Look in hunting catalogs for these and other cost-saving buys. Also, the windsocks are light to carry and add valuable numbers to your flock.

William D. Trout Jr.
Bridgeton, New Jersey

HOW TO BUILD A MOTION STAKE SHELL DECOY

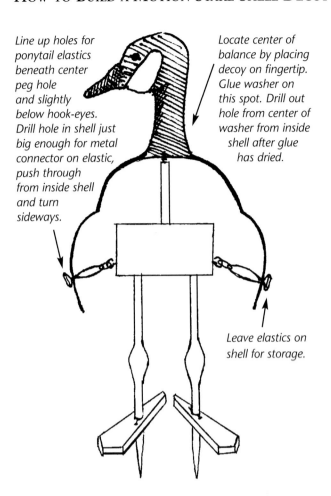

Line up holes for ponytail elastics beneath center peg hole and slightly below hook-eyes. Drill hole in shell just big enough for metal connector on elastic, push through from inside shell and turn sideways.

Locate center of balance by placing decoy on fingertip. Glue washer on this spot. Drill out hole from center of washer from inside shell after glue has dried.

Leave elastics on shell for storage.

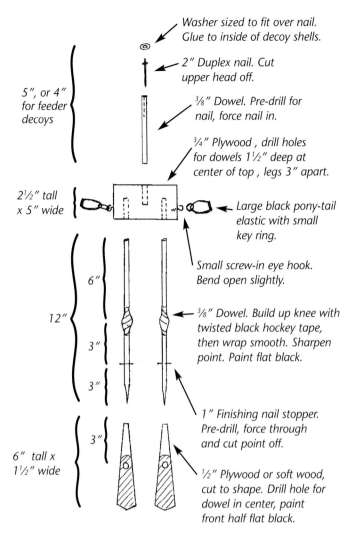

Washer sized to fit over nail. Glue to inside of decoy shells.

2" Duplex nail. Cut upper head off.

⅜" Dowel. Pre-drill for nail, force nail in.

5", or 4" for feeder decoys

¾" Plywood, drill holes for dowels 1½" deep at center of top, legs 3" apart.

2½" tall x 5" wide

Large black pony-tail elastic with small key ring.

Small screw-in eye hook. Bend open slightly.

6"

12"

3"

3"

⅜" Dowel. Build up knee with twisted black hockey tape, then wrap smooth. Sharpen point. Paint flat black.

1" Finishing nail stopper. Pre-drill, force through and cut point off.

6" tall x 1½" wide

3"

½" Plywood or soft wood, cut to shape. Drill hole for dowel in center, paint front half flat black.

LIFELIKE DECOYS

When duck hunting on calm days, your decoy spread will have little movement. A bag of rocks could save the day. Throwing rocks into your decoy spread will create ripples and realistic motion that incoming birds will see. Just don't let the ducks see your movement when you throw the rocks.

Ducks that see movement in a decoy spread are more likely to swing over your spread to investigate. One-inch to 2-inch dark rocks seem to work best, especially in clear, shallow water.

William D. Trout Jr.
Bridgeton, New Jersey

MIX YOUR DECOYS

When hunting with field decoys, mix some silhouette decoys with your shell or full-bodied decoys. As the geese circle, your silhouette decoys will appear and disappear, giving the illusion of movement.

Terry Murray
via e-mail

MARK SHOTGUN SHELLS

I do a lot of upland bird and duck hunting, and I used to have trouble with shells getting mixed up. Now, when I buy a box of shells, the first thing I do is mark the bases by the primer. I use permanent markers. On steel shot, I mark the shot size in black marker across the full size of the base. This way I can see the size easier in low light and don't have to worry if the lettering rubs off the side of the shell. On lead shot, I color the entire base red (red rhymes with lead) and then mark the shot size in black.

On some trips, I used to get shells mixed together and would wind up having some lead with me while duck hunting. I haven't made that mistake since I started marking shells this way.

Joe Maringo
Plum, Pennsylvania

Steel shotshells get black numbering right on the brass.

Lead shotshells get a red base underneath the numbering.

GOOSE SECRETS

When decoying geese over water or land, be patient. Once the geese have cupped their wings and you know they're about to land among your decoys, wait until they're about 6 feet off the water or ground. Pick one bird near the outer limit of your effective shooting range and shoot at its head or neck. Geese will almost always have to land on the water or ground once they drop to within 6 feet or so of it. Then they must compose themselves enough to propel themselves upward after the first shot. This should allow you time to select a second or third bird at closer range than the first.

Richard C. Meyers
Wind Gap, Pennsylvania

CLOTHING REPAIR

For repairing leaks in waders, boots or decoys, use clear RTV silicone adhesive sealant. It does a great job.

Richard Nusser
Morton Grove, Illinois

LEADING BIRDS

When shooting at ducks, goose, pheasants or other game birds, aim for the bird's head with your shotgun. The bird will fly right into the shot pattern. I lost a few good pheasants until I learned this trick.

Seth Dyal
Medford, Oregon

SPECIAL SECTION
GAME BIRD TIPS

CARRY A GUN CASE

When I go hunting with a gun, I always carry a thin, lightweight gun case folded up in my hunting coat. You never know what might happen or where you might end up, and if the chance to catch a ride with someone comes along, you will legally be able to go.

Robert J. Manske
Portage, Wisconsin

"Just in case," carry a lightweight gun case when you hunt.

PREVENTING BLISTERS

One thing I hate when I'm enjoying a great hunt is getting blisters from new boots or even boots that are already broken in. I find if I put a small amount of Armor All in a sandwich-sized zip-top bag and line the heel of my hiking boots with the sealed bag, it creates a gel-like cushion that doesn't take up much space.

Kevin Grant
Farmingdale, Maine

STAY WARM WITH A GROUND COVER

If you do any late-season, cold-weather goose hunting, here is a way to stay toasty warm even on the coldest days. Rather than lying on the cold ground, use a piece of closed-cell foam from a hardware or surplus store, or the seat padding inside a bench seat from a vehicle that has been totaled. The foam insulates you from the cold ground and soaks up some of your own body heat, keeping you almost as warm as if you were still snug in your bed.

John Paczkowski
Bismarck, North Dakota

 PREDATORS

Interest in predator hunting grows by leaps and bounds every year.

It's a whole new world of hunting—to pursue a *predator* (such as a coyote), instead of *prey* (such as a deer or game bird). The rules are different, the rewards still great.

What follows will teach you how to hunt predators right now ... or how to get even better at the game if you already pursue these wariest-of-the-wary animals.

A PREDATOR HUNTING PRIMER

I have been calling coyotes for more than 30 years. I don't know how many I have called in, and I don't really care. I just love to call. Here is what coyotes have taught this old farm boy.

I like mouth calls, although I have an electronic caller for special occasions, such as when I can't get the coyotes to come to a mouth call. I practice mouth calls at home a lot. I listen to a tape, and then try to imitate the sound. It works. It also drives my wife nuts! There are three distinct types of mouth calls: closed metal reed, open reed and diaphragm calls. (See sidebar on page 139).

CALLING SOUNDS

Most calls will sound like a dying rabbit, either a cottontail or jackrabbit. But when these sounds don't work—and there will be times they won't—you must be flexible enough to change.

Try a fawn distress, canine puppy, coyote pup distress or flicker call. I have even called in coyotes with a squealing pig sound.

After coyotes have paired up—usually in January and February— you can switch to howling. It takes quite a bit of practice to imitate the correct sounds to pull

He's cagey, he's cautious … he's a coyote, and hunting him is pure fun.

a coyote in. Don't try it unless you have listened to and can imitate the correct sound. I practice a lone howl on my dog, Katie. She howls along with a territorial howl. Katie gets defensive, growls and leaves the room to get my wife, which usually ends the session. Be sure to practice, otherwise you will get discouraged when nothing comes to the call.

Don't be afraid to switch calls during a setup. Let me tell of an experience I recently had.

A nearby landowner asked me to come over and help deplete his song-dog population. Seems they like eating baby calves a little too much for him. On a still, clear and cold morning, about minus 5°F, I was set up on a large draw. It was very open, with smaller draws feeding into it. We had complete snow cover, which helps in spotting coyotes. I sneaked into the place I wanted to call from, got set up, waited a couple of minutes to get situated, and let things get back to normal.

When I felt comfortable, I began my first series of a dying four-legged short-tailed furball. Within a couple of minutes, I noticed a customer about 400 yards to my left. He trotted in a couple of yards and then stopped. (I hate it when they do that!) I noticed he kept looking across the draw to my left. I figured his partner was doing a sneak on me. Sure enough, a couple of minutes later she appeared, trotting from my left about 120 yards out. I stopped her with a lip squeak, and dropped her where she stood.

Meanwhile, her better half observed all this from afar. I barked to bring him closer. No deal! So I growled, but still no deal. I noticed he was still concentrating on something to my left. I switched tactics and worked a mouse squeaker for about five minutes. Still no deal, but suddenly less than 10 yards in front of me, another coyote appeared. All I could see in the scope was fur, but I squeezed off a shot. She bit at the entry wound and growled.

I looked up to find Mr. Slowpoke on the other side of the draw, now coming at a dead run. Maybe the shot and the growling changed his mind. He soon appeared at the site where the first coyote fell, and that's where he stayed.

Maybe you picked up on another point in that story: Continue to call after you shoot a coyote. Most of the time, coyotes run in pairs or more. There is a good chance to double your take if you have patience. I was done with the triple in less than 20 minutes. One more thing: Learn to lip squeak, click your teeth and growl. Any one of these will normally make a coyote stop. Be ready. That's when you want to shoot.

CALLING TECHNIQUES

Always start off soft, slowly increase the volume to a loud volume and high pitch about halfway through the set, then taper off. A normal set in open country will last 20 to 30 minutes for coyotes. Coyotes are fast, but their hearing is a lot better than ours. If one hears you from 2 or 3 miles away, it might take him 20 minutes to get to you.

In rough, brushy country, the set can be shorter because the sound is drowned out by the landscape. Whatever country you are in, when the calling gets tough in February and March, expect to stay longer on each set. The song dogs will be a lot more cautious about coming in to a call.

Some guys call for about 10 seconds with 5 to 7 short screams. Wait 20 or 30 seconds and do it again. Do this 2 to 3 times for one series, wait five minutes and start again. Other hunters scream

CALLING PREDATORS

You can call in predators by sucking on the back of your hand to sound like an injured rabbit or bird.

Joe Rode
Traverse City, Michigan

MOUTH CALLS

CLOSED METAL REED CALLS

These are easy to find and easy to use. About all you have to do is breathe into the end of it. The metal reed likes to freeze up in cold weather, which can be counteracted by putting a piece of cloth over the end. This helps keep some moisture out of the call. Also, keep it next to your body between setups, to prevent freeze-up.

OPEN REED CALLS

Open reed calls are easy to find and harder to master, but you can make many different sounds with one call. You can change the Mylar reed, if needed, for different sounds. Occasionally the reed will go flat and need replacing.

Closed and open reed calls.

DIAPHRAGM CALLS

These calls work really well for close-up work. You can keep your hands free to shoot. Diaphragm calls also work for medium-distance work. Most of these calls don't last too long, because the latex tends to rot with repeated use. But these calls are inexpensive.

Gene Opbroek
Pickstown, South Dakota

constantly for a minute or more, and then stop, wait and begin again. Both methods work, so do whatever you want. Be flexible if something doesn't work.

Work electronic callers the same way. Some hunters turn them on and off, others just let them scream.

With howling, you must be more patient. Howl and wait. If you get an answer, depending on what it is, you might need to talk back. Or you might need to shut up and wait. I recently lost a coyote because I got too aggressive. I blew a locator call, and this coyote came back with an aggressive bark-howl, so we exchanged pleasantries for a couple minutes. But then the big chicken never showed! Sometimes you can talk them right out of being shot. Whatever call or technique you use, usually a mouse or lip squeak will bring them closer for the shot.

CAMOUFLAGE

The most important thing is to sit still. Imagine someone watching you from 500 yards away with 10-power binoculars. That's how a coyote sees you. You can get by with some slow head movement. Once you see the critter, move only when Mr. Coyote is looking away or down. A coyote will sometimes look down before he starts to move, so be ready to move your gun into position.

I will not look directly at a critter for more than a second, and then it's just to see where they are. I think they have a sixth sense that makes them nervous when you watch them too much.

Don't silhouette yourself. Even when I call while on the South Dakota prairies, I get below the hill's crest. I try to get in front of a bush, tree or yucca plant, or I sit on an old cow trail. Vegetation in front of your set will help if it does not interfere with the shot. If you need to, cut some shooting lanes.

Camouflage clothing is always a good idea. Wear whites when snow covers the ground. It will help get the critter closer. I take every advantage I can get my hot little hands on to take a critter. Camouflage your face and hands. If you're using a mouth call, your hands will be moving. Cover them!

THE SETUP

Sneak in, set up, call and sneak out. Have the attitude that the quarry is watching your every move! It is important to know the landscape. Most coyotes, unless they are starving, stupid or suicidal, will wind you before they get within 30 to 50 yards. With a rifle, this usually isn't a problem, unless they have been burned by a hunk of lead. With a rifle, you want to take them before they get within 50 yards. They get mighty big, even at 3-power on the scope, when they get closer than that.

Coyotes will use the easiest, safest, most direct route to get to the call, while using wind and landscape to their advantage. Set up to use the wind and land to your advantage. Give the critter a chance to use a draw to wind you, and then shoot him as he goes to that spot. Use cow trails, fencelines, the end of cornfields and so on to give him an approach avenue he feels comfortable with.

Take a low-impact approach to your coyote hunting.

Then set up so you can shoot to that avenue. A good friend of mine just started hunting coyotes with me. Jeff has hunted deer all of his life, but he's getting a passion for coyotes. The first time I took him, he kept looking for coyotes in the bottom of the draws. He wasn't prepared for them to come over the top of the ridge. Watch everywhere. They will appear like ghosts, and what a thrill when they do!

A short note on wind. The best wind is about 10 to 15 mph, which helps set up that avenue of approach by letting you somewhat predict where the critter will go. If I'm calling for any old coyote, I set up with a crosswind or the wind in my face. If I am calling to get Mr. Wile E., I use a cover scent and call with the wind at my back. That takes much persistence, patience and skill. You have to know the habits of your quarry and be prepared to sit still for more than 30 minutes, with only your

eyeballs moving. Offer something he hasn't had, let him wind you, and you still might have to make a 250-yard-plus shot. If the wind is blowing faster than 20 mph, stay home or call into it as loud as possible. Make your sets shorter and much closer together. Remember, sound does not travel far in strong winds.

With a wind less than 15 mph, have a friend walk away from you as you blow on a call. Tell him to stop when he can no longer hear you. Multiply the distance times 8. That is how much better a coyote can hear, and that is about how far the sound travels. Furthermore, the more hills, trees and brush, the less distance the sound travels.

Get into a set routine. Here's mine: First, I use the landscape to get to the setup without being heard or seen. I find a spot with good camouflage where I won't be silhouetted. The site must be comfortable, have good shooting lanes and provide

Sneak in carefully, set up quietly, call effectively, sneak back out.

an avenue of approach for my quarry. When I sit down, preferably with my back against something, I put the Remington on my shooting sticks or a bipod, check my shooting lanes and decide where I'll take the shot if a coyote comes in. I set my shooting sticks close to my body, with my riflescope almost under my armpit. I do this because then I can rest my arms on the rifle and shooting sticks. This way, I eliminate the movement of my arms bringing the call to my mouth, and it is more comfortable.

I pull out the call I am going to use, check it and make sure I'm going to blow into the right end. Then I jack a round into the Remington,

THE GUN

Know where your gun shoots. I use a 20-year-old Remington Model 78 in .22-250. It has a Weaver 3-9X variable scope, and I use shooting sticks for every shot. I use moly-coated ballistic-tip ammo with a 40- or 55-grain bullet. I have to set a new zero if I switch from 55- to 40-grain bullets. I'm dialed in to hit 2 inches high at 100 yards, which puts me dead on at 200 yards. If I put it on the top of a coyote's back between 200 and 450 yards, the animal dies.

Almost any high-stepping small-caliber rifles will work. This includes the .22-250, .222, .220 Swift or .243 if you want to save fur. Otherwise, almost anything you can hit a coyote with will work. For shots inside 50 yards, a 10 or 12 gauge shotgun with No. 2 shot can be used, especially if two of you are hunting, one with a rifle, the other with a shotgun.

Gene Opbroek
Pickstown, South Dakota

More important than the caliber or make of your predator hunting rifle is your ability to shoot it accurately out to 200-plus yards (top). A shotgun (bottom) makes a wonderful close-in predator gun when loaded with No. 2 shot. Carry two guns to your setup so that you're ready for either scenario. Or, if hunting with a partner, one person should be the shotgunner. You'll be surprised at how many close encounters happen in coyote hunting; that's where the shotgun shines.

check my watch and wait about five minutes to let nature get back to normal after my invasion. Then I begin to call. After I am done, I sneak back out the same way I came in.

The Shot

Say what you want, but a coyote is not a big target. Besides that, they're tough. Do everything possible to avoid poorly placed shots. Wait for coyotes to turn sideways, if possible. When they turn, they are not coming any closer. Give a lip squeak and when they stop, shoot. At best, a large coyote is about 12 inches across the chest, with 4 inches of it being fur.

I do not like frontal shots. The percentages are against me making a good shot. If you make a bad shot, be patient. If left alone, the coyote will run over the next hill and, if hit well enough, will lie down and die. If it isn't hit hard, a shot at a scared coyote is a low-percentage shot. The next time you hunt him, he will be a scholar, and will probably hang up at 400 yards—or not come at all unless you change calls and tactics. For these reasons, take only high-percentage shots or wait for a better opportunity.

Show Courtesy, Gain Admittance

In all the years I have hunted coyotes on private property, I have only been turned down by a landowner once. That was because his son hunted coyotes. I grew up on a farm in the Midwest. I understand the relationship between the land and the landowner. I have chased cows, fixed fences, delivered calves, picked up parts in town and many other small chores that meant a lot to the landowners who let me hunt.

I refuse to hunt with those who break game laws, and I haven't lost any friends because of it. My friends will not put me in that situation, and the folks who do are not friends, hunters or conservationists. If I have a question on a game law, I call a game warden for clarification. When a new game warden moves into the area, I meet him and try to build a healthy relationship.

Doubles are common in coyote hunting. If you shoot one dog, stick around awhile and see if you can coax his partner in.

Regarding Traditions

I am proud of the hunting traditions my father taught me. I strive to make quick, clean kills; I retrieve all game I kill; and I only kill what I intend to use. I also strive to respect the laws, the land and my fellow hunter.

I am also proud to be a Life Member of the North American Hunting Club. The ethics and morals portrayed by this organization are those taught by my father and his father before him. Thank you for letting that tradition continue.

Gene Opbroek
Pickstown, South Dakota

TIPS FOR THE BEGINNING
COYOTE CALLER

The number of coyotes across America continues to grow. With no closed season in many parts of the country, there is hunting to be done all year long. Calling coyotes is one of the most challenging and entertaining forms of hunting. This sport will enhance and challenge every hunting skill you've ever learned. All you really need is a call, some camouflage and a little time. But there are some basic skills and tricks you'll need to know to become consistently successful.

The coyote is an intelligent and resourceful animal that never ceases to amaze me with its hardiness as a predator. If you are going to become a proficient coyote caller, you'd better have your game face on every time you go afield, or you'll only be moderately successful. To consistently call in coyotes, you need to pay attention to details and be prepared for the coyote's every move.

TIP 1: LOCATION, LOCATION, LOCATION

One of the best things coyote hunters can do is get to know their hunting area intimately. Buy topographical maps of the area you plan to hunt, scout the area thoroughly for sign and select good calling sites. In order to call coyotes, there must be coyotes in the area you plan to hunt. Drive back roads, talk to ranchers and their hands, and walk promising areas to locate sign. Use your topographical map to mark the areas that look good and the best locations to call from. Pay special attention to wind direction and make sure you have a good field of view.

Be cautious of having so much cover that you can't see the coyote until he's standing next to you. Too much cover can also allow him to get downwind of you without you ever seeing him. The coyote's nose is as good as any animal's in the

Coyote hunting is fun, but it's also a detail game. Pay attention to all details of every hunt if you want to be successful.

wild. Always set up with the wind in your face or, at least, at a crosswind. Later, you can use the map to mark areas where you've had success. Over time, you will notice trends about the type of areas that consistently produce coyotes.

Many calling setups are ruined before a call is ever blown. If you can't get into the selected calling site without being seen or heard, you'll never have much success. I believe a quiet, unseen approach to a calling site will yield more coyotes than any other technique a hunter can use.

Once you've scouted an area and approached your calling site without being seen or heard, you have to make the coyote believe he needs to come and either greet you or eat you.

TIP 2: QUALITY CALLING

Nothing in the wild dies easily. So why do some people call as if it's a mundane, routine ordeal? Some hunters would lead us to believe that if we make a simple waa-waa-waa sound, coyotes will come running. Maybe some will come, but not as many as if you put some emotion into your calling. Always try to imagine you're a rabbit and a coyote is trying to eat you. This simple thought will remind you of the emotion you should have in your calling sounds. Remember: The amount of emotion we call with has nothing to do with how loudly we call.

Always begin a calling sequence with soft calling, so you don't frighten coyotes close to you. Wailing out a loud sequence of calls to a coyote that is bedded only a few hundred yards away or less will send it running for the hills. If you've done your part and approached your calling location carefully, you'll be surprised how many times a coyote comes in immediately. You might even spot him before you start to call. After your initial sequence, wait a minute or two before you begin another sequence. This gives you the opportunity to scan the area for a customer.

The type of call you use is not as important as how you use it. There are so many high-quality calls on the market today, the coyote caller could use any of them and be successful. For the beginner, a tape, CD or chip-caller is a good choice.

Get into your calling spot and set up without being seen or heard.

Call with emotion and you'll pull in more coyotes.

They require no practice to make the right sounds and there are a variety of sounds available. Be sure you select the sound of an animal found in your hunting area. Hand-held calls are more versatile than mechanical calls because they allow the caller to adapt to the actions of the coyote. Being able to react to what a coyote is doing can be critical at times. It can be the difference between an educated coyote and a dead one.

TIP 3: SET UP RIGHT & BE READY

Being ready begins when you select your stand location. A stand location provides good visibility and cover without cutting off your ability to maneuver your rifle, bow or shotgun. Simple things like having your gun or bow in a position where little or no movement is required to take the shot when it's available are part of being ready.

No two coyotes approach a caller exactly the same way. I've been hunting coyotes for more than 25 years, and they never cease to amaze me with their actions.

But there are certain clues about what a coyote

Once you're set up, be alert and ready at all times.

might do next. Seasoned coyote hunters learn to recognize these clues and use them to their advantage. For instance, if a coyote comes into a call and suddenly turns sideways within 200 yards and trots parallel to you while looking in your direction, he suspects something is up. This dog will turn and leave or try to circle downwind of you. Take the first good shot. If a coyote comes within a few hundred yards, sits down and looks in your direction or at the area around you, he might still come in, but you should carefully examine the area. Many times, this means another coyote has approached without you seeing him, and is nearby. The incoming coyote is sizing up his competition for a meal, or he's waiting to see what happens.

On the other hand, if the coyote stops suddenly or turns away and looks back, he's spotted something he didn't like and is going to leave. Some coyotes come in at a full run and never stop. This can be a real problem. The caller who is not prepared to take the shot generally watches as a gray streak goes right on by or slams on the brakes and leaves as fast as it came. Have your weapon ready for action and you'll be able to put some of these wily critters on the ground. Carry a shotgun for the close-in shots.

Over time, you'll be able to recognize what a coyote might do next. There will always be times when you end up shaking your head and laughing at yourself. So be sure you have a good deal of humility. If you don't, Mr. Coyote will be sure to give you some.

CONCLUSION

Volumes have been written on how to be a better coyote caller. I'd suggest you read every book, listen to every tape and watch every video you can. The more you learn, the better off you'll be. The only trick to calling lots of coyotes is getting out in the field and doing it as much as possible. The best knowledge you can get is gained from the lessons a coyote teaches you.

Ronald Bryant
North Las Vegas, Nevada

LITTLE SECRETS FOR PREDATOR CALLERS

• Hang a film canister or other scent distributor from a tree or bush downwind of your calling site. Placing the scent above ground allows wind currents to carry the scent more effectively. The scents I've found most effective for predators have been rabbit or skunk. In areas that hold good fox numbers, it is also effective as an attractant and as a cover scent.

• For a simple decoy, use a large feather tied by dental floss or other light thread to a bush near your calling location. This is often enough to catch an incoming predator's attention and give you a chance to position yourself for a shot. This technique is super-effective for bobcats, because sight is their number one asset used to locate prey. If you have to expose yourself to the area in order to hang the feather, don't use it. It's not worth ruining a calling site. The feather also works great when attached to a foam rabbit decoy's ear. It seems to get the eyes of the predator fixated to the decoy by increasing its movement.

• When setting up to call, always try to sit on the shaded side of cover. The distorted light will significantly enhance the effectiveness of your camouflage. Ensure that you blend into your background cover and you don't have anything in front of you to block your vision or inhibit your movement.

• The new seats designed for turkey hunting are also great for the predator caller. These seats are lightweight and have self-supporting backs. They make setting up to call a lot more comfortable, and you don't have to worry about your tail end getting poked by sharp rocks and other things.

• Sew some elastic loops, like the ones used to hold shotgun shells on hunting vests, to your favorite hunting coat or shirt. The loops of elastic will hold your calls on a lanyard ready for use, and they won't clack together to make noise while you're sneaking to your calling site.

• When selecting a calling site, choose an elevated location. Many predators don't look up when running or trotting into a call, especially coyotes. They tend to run with their eyes focused on the ground in front of them. This might be to make sure they don't step on something painful, but it works to your advantage for spotting the incoming predator and moving your weapon for the shot.

Ronald Bryant
North Las Vegas, Nevada

The author with the results of one predator population reduction project.

SMALL GAME

Rabbits and squirrels don't get much press, but hunters sure love them.

Of course, small game is perfect for the young and beginning hunter. But those of us beyond the "starting out" stage—even if it's been decades—can learn from the simplicity and joy that goes with hunting rabbits and squirrels again.

Don't forget your hunting roots. Visit them sometimes. Give a young hunter the opportunities you had. That's what small game hunting is about.

RABBIT RUN

We had planned this weekend for many weeks. Deer season had been over since early January, and we were itching to go to the woods if for nothing but a good camp-out.

It was Easter weekend, and we had three days to get the camp ready for the next season's deer hunt. We planned to do a little squirrel hunting, and rabbit was fair game also. My son, Aaron, a typical five-year-old, was always ready to go, and since he had been on hunting trips since he was old enough to walk, I really looked forward to taking him.

The work around the camp took a lot of time, and we hadn't found much spare time to do much serious hunting. We had settled on maybe a few squirrels, or possibly even a coyote, which there had been plenty of during deer season. Other than a lot of hard work, we saw very little of anything "gamy."

Easter morning came, and to Aaron's amazement, the Easter Bunny had made a deep-woods delivery: a basket full of all types of Easter goodies.

This particular morning seemed to be the best of the previous three. We had a light frost on the ground, which for that part of Texas was highly unusual. I knew this was the morning to go. Besides that, we had to leave for home later that morning.

Aaron and I went through the ritual of getting ready at least an hour before sunup, and nothing but full camo was good enough for my son. After all, he knew it was at least seven months until the next hunt. During my deer hunting trips, I had seen an old barn area with a storm shelter. Everything was gone except for the corner posts of

It was Easter morning. Was the rabbit the Easter Bunny ... or just another everyday cottontail?

the barn and a concrete stairwell in the middle of an open field. Old pecan trees grew in that area, and I had high hopes for at least a few squirrels.

We walked a good half mile to the area, crept through the field and headed to the tree line. Aaron had an eerie feeling that something was in that stairwell, and being that I'd actually never been up close to look at it, I thought it was worth our while to take a look.

Aaron was really excited, and with a mouth full of Easter candy, he was at the height of his short but action-packed hunting career. I wasn't expecting to see anything at all.

We walked to the base of the stairwell and looked in. A fine cottontail jumped at our feet and headed anywhere but there. I was carrying a 12 gauge and put a bead on him as he zigzagged across the open field. A cottontail of that size in that part of Texas is rare. Jackrabbits are the regular.

He ran about 20 yards and came to a complete halt, just as expected. I sat the bead right on him. It was an easy shot.

About then, I felt a distinct tug on my shirtsleeve. Aaron was doing the tugging. I knew that we had been together on numerous hunts, but this was different. I didn't feel right. I leaned the muzzle toward the ground. The rabbit just sat there and looked at us like he knew what day it was, and I didn't say anything, but I knew Aaron knew that it was the "Easter Bunny."

Aaron immediately said that the trees we were hunting for were over there, and that was where we headed. We had a great time in that tree line. We saw "plenty squirrel," but we never saw a rabbit again.

We picked up camp and headed back home, and even though that was one trip we didn't get a rabbit, Aaron knew that was his first "shot not taken."

William Sandlin Jr.
Houston, Texas

RABBIT CARRYING MADE EASY

While rabbit hunting, carrying several rabbits can be difficult. Louisiana marsh rabbits can grow to more than twice the size of an average cottontail. Snowshoe hare hunters will appreciate this tip too.

Hunting vests are good for no more than two large rabbits. I've lost rabbits from using vests that weren't big enough. When I was a kid, my father showed me a simple way to carry rabbits on my belt while hunting. Here it is: Make a 1-inch cut through the back of the rear leg, parallel to the leg and just above the heel between the leg bone and the strap of tough tendon running down to the heel. From the inside, insert the other rear foot through the cut until the heel passes through the cut. Run your belt through the two legs and let the rabbit hang head down from your belt. The weight of the rabbit will keep the feet locked for a good hold until you're ready to field dress your kill.

Gregory M. Guinta
Metairie, Louisiana

RABBIT CLEANING MADE EASY

When dressing rabbits, cut through the sternum to the neck, and then down from the sternum to the anal opening. Keep the sharp part of the knife away from the internal organs to avoid punctures. Be sure no one is behind you for this next step: Grab the rabbit tightly by its two front feet and snap it backward briskly. Most of the internal organs will fly out behind you.

Richard Nusser
Morton Grove, Illinois

MEMORIES OF MY FATHER SQUIRREL HUNTING

AND OTHER LESSONS FROM THE WOODLOTS OF AUTUMN

My first hunting memories involve squirrel hunting. I wasn't old enough to hunt, but I was old enough to know that my father did. And already I liked the idea of hunting.

I would wait expectantly at home, imagining the big adventures that were going on out there in the wooded hills outside of town … without me. And then I'd kick another field goal over the old, rusty swingset next to the apple tree in our backyard.

Even then, football was only something to entertain yourself and bide time when you couldn't be hunting.

But when my father came home, all was better. I remember hugging him not only because I missed him, but also to find out what he got and especially to smell the autumn woods on his clothes.

He would send me to the trunk of the old Impala, where I would pull

A fox squirrel trophy.

out the worn, faded brown canvas hunting jacket and extract the squirrels inside. Usually a mix of grays and big rust-colored fox squirrels, I'd study them intently, drink in the forest smells emanating from their fur, and dream of the day when I too would be a squirrel hunter.

Eventually that day came. But I had an apprenticeship first.

I am not an old person, but neither am I young anymore. I am in the middle somewhere, and I grew up in a place and time where hunting—yes, even of squirrels—was an accepted practice, a common autumn pastime, and even considered a good way to keep young boys on the straight and narrow.

I remember walking in the bare woods that November day, thinking I'd never felt air so cold or alive. Looking back, it was probably just a brisk day. Maybe the shaking was the excitement of being hunting. This was one of my birthday presents— being here, in the woods at last.

Dad shot a squirrel high, high up in an oak tree and after it tumbled down with a satisfying "thump," I carried it by the tail the rest of the day, trying to be quiet but not doing too good a job at it. We would have been better off in the soft woods of October. But November's orange light was special late that afternoon as we walked down the railroad tracks back to our car.

It was the best birthday present I ever received.

The statute of limitations has surely run out on this one, but: I shot my first squirrel a couple years later, well before I was old enough to have a license, after my Dad handed me his ancient and scarred but deadly-accurate bolt-action .22. "Only shoot them in the head," he said. And I did, leaning over his shoulder as he knelt down to give me a steady rest for the shot.

It felt different, picking up something I had killed, and my father left me alone there for awhile with the big, bushy-tailed gray squirrel, amidst the glory of October's woods and the emotions filling my heart.

Of course, I went on to hunt many more squirrels at my father's side before I completed hunter safety training and reached the magic age of 12 when I could carry my own single-shot .22. And during this apprenticeship my dad often seemed more than happy to let me do the shooting.

That happens when you get to the age that he was then and I am now. The killing is the least part of the hunt. Being there, family ... those are the things that matter.

I remember the clothes my father wore squirrel hunting.

He wore faded jeans, "denim blue fading up to the sky" as Cat Stevens sang in one of his songs of the day. Leather work boots carried my father up and down those southwestern Wisconsin hills. The old, faded canvas jacket—shrunken from far too many washings—was always on top, except for warm days when a lightweight hunting vest replaced it.

Now that I look back, I can see that the outfit was the best that could be done for quiet woods-sneaking, in those days before miraculously quiet fabrics hit yet-to-be-created sporting goods catalogs and megastores. Old jeans don't scritch and scratch against berry vines, tree bark, bushes and other noisemakers. The canvas jacket had been pummeled into soft submission in my mother's washing machine, and was similarly quiet. The boots were sturdy, well oiled, comfortable and broken in. A brown Jones hat topped off the attire.

But what I remember most is the old flannel shirt. How I wish I had that shirt now.

Blue-and-white checked, soft as could be, sleeves rolled up ... I can see Dad leaning against a hickory tree now, scanning the woods ahead for a squirrel working the limbs of an oak, hickory or walnut tree.

IMITATING A SQUIRREL

To calm a squirrel after shooting, or to lure a squirrel to move, rub two coins together between your fingers to imitate the sound of a squirrel eating a nut.

Sam George
Brunswick, Maryland

Rub two quarters together to sound like a squirrel eating a nut.

TRICKING A SQUIRREL

To attract squirrels for an easy shot, tap two empty shotgun shells together, or tap the wooden stock of your gun a few times with your knuckle. It works!

Joe Rode
Traverse City, Michigan

A little tapping (use empty shells) can attract curious squirrels.

But I suppose like so many other things in life, it wore out and got repaired too many times before finally reaching the stage where it wasn't worth saving anymore.

Yet no matter what it looked like, I would wear it out into the woods once or twice a year today. And if it couldn't bear that wear, I would just keep it in a box somewhere.

Sometimes the things we think aren't worth saving become the things that matter the most.

For a year, my family lived in Browntown, a tiny burg of 200 or so people in the valley of the mighty Pecatonica River. From anywhere in town, you could see off into the hills, some of the most beautiful hills anywhere. In those days, if you didn't shoot cows, you could hunt pretty much where you wanted.

On an October day, when the color-filled woodlots alternated with green hayfields and tan cornfields all the way to the horizon, the beautiful hills must have beckoned to my father. And they are lovely, still some of the loveliest hills I have ever seen, and I have climbed many others since then.

Dad was the depot agent in town, and if the train had come through and the paperwork was done, he would shut down the train office early, walk two blocks home, change into his hunting clothes and head for the hills.

I was in school, not home yet, and I never got too upset that Dad had gone hunting without me. Saturdays and Sundays were for that. Plus, in some precocious way, I think I realized that Dad needed his time alone in those woods too. Just like I need some time alone in woods now.

He told me of a squirrel, "a huge old hook-nosed fox squirrel" as he described it, that lived in a

Fat gray squirrels occupied many hunting dreams.

pasture woods atop a ridge above town. No matter how Dad tried, he could not get that squirrel. Sneak in over the top, creep up from the bottom, crawl along on the contour of the hill … with only 10 or 15 big white oaks for cover in the whole place (perfect fox squirrel country), the old master could not be approached.

So, one perfect autumn day as my dad described it, he left work at 2:00 instead of 3:00, climbed the ridge and lay down under one of the trees the squirrel preferred for his afternoon feeding session. Like clockwork, the big old bull squirrel showed up, and he was reduced to Sunday dinner.

Dad told me he felt bad about finally killing that squirrel. I didn't understand the reasons then. But I know now. Yet, my father still found plenty of reasons to haul himself—and his son—up into the oak and hickory woodlots that taught not so much about the killing of squirrels as they did the value of special places and special relationships of both the father-son and hunter-hunted variety.

There came a day when I earned my hunter safety certificate, got a hunting license, and carried my own single-shot .22 into the woods I had already come to love. We hunted together then, or very close to each other, and the mix of security and independence was good for a growing boy.

Then, after a couple years, on the evening before squirrel season's Opening Day, Dad laid out a plan. We would each hunt a different woodlot the next morning, and meet up at 9:00 or so in the "walnut woods" pasture that ran between the two forests.

Dawn came slowly the next morning in the fog as I waited alone, in the gray, probably too early for any squirrels to be out anyway. Yet as the fog lifted slowly, the woods came to life. When the sun peeked out and lit up the day, I was in the middle of squirrel heaven and I think my father knew that would be the case.

Within an hour, I had taken five shots, and two big grays and three huge fox squirrels pulled my gamebag low and hurt my shoulders—a limit! I walked out to the walnut woods early. Dad was there too: Had he even hunted or was he just waiting for me? October's color was just gearing up, and we met in the green-and-yellow timber.

"I heard five shots," Dad said. And I proudly pulled the squirrels out one by one and laid them on the sun-dappled tractor trail there in the walnut woods. Dad examined them carefully one by one, each bigger than the other and each shot once in the noggin where they had no chance of getting away.

"Oh, that's good," he said, smiling and patting me on the back.

With the wisdom of a few years behind me, and kids of my own, I can now see my father's plan for that day. It worked. I graduated. And I have since received a fancy degree or two from schools much more prestigious than the rolling hills of southwestern Wisconsin.

But I can also say that no other graduation meant as much, made me feel as good, or taught me as much about life, family, doing things right and being independent, as that day in the Green County hills.

My father is the best teacher I ever had.

We still hunt together, chasing deer in that same country. And I have even taken him out after turkeys, now that they have been reintroduced and are thriving in the beautiful hills, and we have found success there too.

But the squirrels seem to take a back seat. Dad doesn't chase them on his own anymore because the hills are too steep to climb. And when I find time to break away from the busy-ness called life today and make the long drive back and we hunt together, our sights are set on the bigger and more glamorous game that can be hunted sitting still.

But I feel good that we just hunt together, even now, after these many years … that we find time in

fall, that season of seasons, to be side by side in the land in which I grew up and he grew old.

We still see the squirrels out there, and we talk about hunting them one more time together. I don't know if either of us could bear to shoot one though. And that's fine. Soon enough, perhaps, there will be some of my offspring out there to do it in our stead. And I will teach them like my father taught me.

And in the end, that's the whole idea, isn't it?

Tom Carpenter
Plymouth, Minnesota

ONE BOY'S WAY TO SKIN A SQUIRREL

I'm only 15 and I haven't been hunting for long, but I taught myself an excellent way to skin squirrels. Most people I've watched skin a squirrel start by cutting a slit up the stomach and then cutting around the body. I start by cutting a slit underneath the squirrel's tail, and then I cut through the tailbone. Next, I step on the tail while grabbing the squirrel by the hind legs and pulling up.

This method takes off most of the skin except for some on the legs, which can be easily removed by shaving off the skin with your knife; or grab the tip of the "V" of remaining skin with a pliers and pull up. This method works well, and if you're careful you can even keep the squirrel's tail intact.

Perry J. Ekas, age 15
Cabot, Pennsylvania

A TRICK FOR TAKING BUSHYTAILS

When you are walking through the woods and a squirrel spots you, it often runs up a tree and starts barking. If you want a shot, here is what you can do. Take off your shirt or jacket and hang it up on a tree limb. Now take your time to creep around to the side of the tree where the squirrel is hiding. The bushytail will still be looking at the shirt or jacket. Now you can take your shot and add the squirrel to your bag. Good luck trying this tip. I have been really lucky doing this.

Danny Smith
Hughesville, Maryland

SEEK RABBITS IN SUMAC

Sumac bark has a high fat content and is a favorite of rabbits, especially when they are under the stress of winter. Check out all sumac thickets carefully when hunting winter rabbits.

James Matousek
Herkimer, New York

A LINE ON CLOTHING REPAIR

Hunting clothing is probably subject to more wear and tear than most apparel. When I need to sew on buttons or repair tears, I use monofilament fishing line. It does not rot and it seldom breaks.

Richard Nusser
Morton Grove, Illinois

SPECIAL SECTION
SMALL GAME TIPS

IMPROVE YOUR HUNTS WITH A JOURNAL

Even if you're not an accomplished writer, keeping a journal of your hunting trips can be beneficial and enjoyable. I take a blank book and keep a log of every hunting trip I take. I include items such as weather, game sightings, friends and family, the location I'm hunting that day, what worked and what didn't.

In a few short seasons you will find yourself going back and reading your entries before the season to get you excited and to aid in preseason scouting. Hunting partners will often refer to the journal just for the memories, and end-of-the-day journal entries will become a topic of discussion as you decide what makes the journal and what doesn't.

In the off-season, I refer back to the journal and place dots on a topographical map showing where I saw game that season. After a few years, the maps make good companions to your journals.

Chris Tennant
Pullman, Washington

Keep a journal to help you remember hunts past ... and plan adventures to come.

GAME-CLEANING GLOVES

I carry a pair of household rubber gloves in my hunting coat or vest inside a plastic bag. They are handy when cleaning game in the field. Place the bloody gloves back in the bag when you finish field dressing game. They are easily washed when you return home. The gloves also keep your hands warm and dry when wrapping decoy anchors after a duck hunt.

Richard Nusser
Morton Grove, Illinois

Make and take your own game-cleaning kit. Include some wipes too, if you want.

CLEANING SQUIRRELS WITH SHEARS

When I was younger, I used to hunt squirrels a lot. Squirrel season was the first to open, and I wanted to be out hunting. I didn't want to waste the game, but I dreaded having to clean them. Later, I even stopped hunting them because it was so difficult to clean them with a knife—the only method I knew and which was the same way I cleaned rabbits. Cleaning took a long time and wasn't worth the effort required to undress the little critter.

Recently, I found that game scissors work wonders on squirrels. Start by clipping off the feet at the first knuckle, then cutting off the head. Next, pinch together a small amount of fur and skin, running from head to tail, in the middle of the back. With the scissors, cut the skin apart enough to allow getting two fingers into the skin. This is the only time hair can get on the meat. Then start pulling the skin apart in opposite directions,

head to tail. Once down to the tail, cut it off from the inside. As one end of the skin comes off the body, grasp the body in the empty hand and continue to remove the rest of the skin. It peels right off the legs and, with no feet in the way, is easily removed.

Now use the scissors to cut into the body cavity, opening the chest to the neck and the tail. With the squirrel open end to end, pull out the intestines and internal organs. After a quick rinse, the process is done. I've found the best scissors to use are made by Chicago Cutlery. They're made from stainless steel and can be taken apart for a thorough cleaning. Also, one blade is notched, which allows for better cutting of the bones.

Now squirrels are again on my most-wanted list. They're good to eat, but that's another story.

Warren S. Everett
Mikado, Michigan

INDEX

Rifles
  barrel rain/snow protection, 108, 121
  coyote hunting, 142
  emergency gun cleaning kit, 91
  gun vise for, 95
  information to file in case of lost/stolen, 119
  moose hunting, 93
  oiling barrel, 54
  practicing shooting with pellet rifle, 19
  sighting in tips, 53, 121
Rifle sling
  antler buttons for, 67
  round-ball compass as stopper for, 123
  sling stopper, 106
Rut hunting
  hunting all day during rut, 43

S

Safety
  building your own gun safe, 31
  emergency signal whistle, 118
  hunting partners and, 23
Scent attractants
  casting deer scent from treestand, 56
  coyote hunting, 147
  deer hunting tips, 11
  gathering scent in field, 58
  heated scent canister, 64
  pill bottle scent container, 67
Scent control
  activated charcoal tablets, 39
  baking soda tips, 39, 66, 97
  chlorophyll tablets, 39
  deer hair as cover scent, 59
  deer hunting tips for, 39
  fresh pine scent, 67
  latex gloves for, 41
  liquid smoke for, 99
  old suitcase to treat clothing, 65
  plastic tubs for, 68
  towel scent-free, 65
  turkey hunting, 74
  unscented baby wipes, 108
Scopes, 74
  spotting scope handle, 101
Scouting
  deer hunting and best time for, 52
  in-home scouting, 116
  one-day strategy for deer, 28
  thread across trail tip, 58
  tips for spotting more game, 114–115
  turkey hunting, 81
Shooting glasses, 129
Shooting rests
  handgun bipod, 106
  tree steps for, 42
Shooting skills/tips
  archery target, 119
  calm, yardage, anchor, focus, release strategy, 42–43
  coyote hunting, 143
  goose hunting, 134

inexpensive bow target, 55
kids' shooting box, 33
one-shot practice sessions for, 38
patterning shotgun, 73
picture-perfect target practice, 102
practicing shooting with pellet rifle, 19
shooting practice on deer shape, 55
shot placement for deer hunting, 11
sighting in, 121
Shotguns
  choke tube holder, 131
  patterning, 73
  preparing to use tips, 72–73
Sighting in rifle, 121
  quick and easy, 53
Sights
  fiber-optic, 74
  iron, 74–75, 122
  open, 74
  perpendicular crosshairs for, 95
  scopes, 74
  spotting scope handle, 101
Skinning frame, 105
Slate call, 81
Snorting for whitetail deer, 40–41
Squirrel hunting
  cleaning squirrels with shears, 157
  making squirrel sounds, 153
  Memories of My Father Squirrel Hunting story, 152–155
  skinning squirrels, 155
  sumac in winter hunting, 156
  trick for taking bushytails, 156
Stalking
  moose hunting, 94

T

Tagging tips
  big game hunting, 106
  low-damage ear tag for deer, 58
Thermos sock, 60
Tracking
  binoculars to trail deer, 48
  in ferns, 108
  foaming spray for blood trail, 49, 108
  quick tracking tip, 60
Treestands
  artificial Christmas tree branches for, 56
  carpeting, 39
  casting deer scent from treestand, 56
  clear shooting lanes from, 56
  green tape to mark trail to, 52
  hiding stand tip, 61
  keeping warm in, 54
  organizing, 62
  retractable dog leash as hoist line, 55
  right height for, 61
  shooting rests for, 42
  sun direction and location for, 28
  triple-purpose treestand rope, 66
  Vaseline quiets seat, 37
  walking to, 39

Trophy mounts
  cleaning, 107
  creating turkey hunt memento, 75
  making your own European mount, 46–47
Turkey hunting
  ABCs of, 86
  beating turkey fever, 75
  Birth of a Turkey Hunter story, 76–77
  in Black Hills, South Dakota, 24–25
  boil and pluck method for cleaning turkeys, 73
  box call, 78, 81
  Brotherly Love in the Turkey Woods story, 79
  calling, 81
  camouflage for turkey hunting, 83
  creating turkey hunt memento, 75
  decoys, 77, 86, 87
  duck calls for, 85
  flushing birds from feeding area for fall turkeys, 87
  judging distance, 75
  late-season and late-in-day hunting, 82–83
  lining up sights, 74–75
  lost call, 81
  in Michigan's late season, 20–22
  mouth call, 81
  patterning, 73
  pellet size for, 73
  persistence pays off for, 84–85
  positioning for, 73–74
  preparing for, 72–73
  scent control, 74
  scouting, 81
  shells for, 73
  slate call, 78, 81
  turkeys as smart vs. dumb, 80–81
  twist ties and field dressing, 87

W

Walking stick, 95
Weather. *See also* Wind
  whitetails in bad weather, 44–45
Whistle
  emergency signal whistle, 118
Wind
  chalk for tracking, 64
  coyote hunting, 141
  deer hunting tips, 39, 65
  feather to detect direction of, 120
  monitoring with thread tied to arrow, 53
  still-hunt with cross-wind, 45
  whitetails in bad weather, 44–45
Women hunting
  bowhunting, 26–27